ANGELS
IN
PARADISE
SHORES OF ETERNITY

ANGELS IN
PARADISE
MUSIC CD
ENCLOSED

FREDDY HAYLER

The "No Ghostwriter" Pledge

Golden Altar Records is an independent publisher with a big heart for God. Although we do not have the luxury of large staffs of corporate researchers and writers at our disposal, there is some advantage to this since this author was all the more dependent on prayer and the grace of God to complete this book! The author acknowledges that he is the sole writer of this book. No other writers have been used in any of the *Song of Angels* series.

Dedication

All glory to the King of heaven and the King of angels, the Lord Jesus Christ!

If a Christian family is but an "earlier heaven," it is because of a godly Christian wife! Thanks, Anne, for your fervent love for the Lord, for me, and for our children. God has made you the perfect soul mate. I dedicate this book to you. I would also like to thank my two lovely daughters, Lindsay and Rebekah. Rebekah, thanks for all the typing—I owe you both a pizza!

What People Are Saying about the Song of Angels series

Have you ever gazed out the window of an airplane into a sea of clouds, or lay on your back in the grass on a lazy summer afternoon watching the clouds float by? If there were music in those clouds, how would it sound? Freddy Hayler offers us a taste of that aerial symphony. Brilliantly combining majestic melodies that stir the soul with lyrics that stir the spirit, *Song of Angels* takes the listener on a journey to the heavenlies. Relax, picture that lazy summer afternoon, and listen to and read the *Song of Angels*."

—Bob Weiner, Evangelist
Youth Now Ministries

I love to listen to his music and hear his message and be there when he worships in his own inimitable style."

—Tommy Tenney
Evangelist
Author of *The God Chasers*

A fresh, new sound of heaven with a powerful, prophetic message best describes this new project entitled *Song of Angels*. True worship was never intended to be an entertainment media, but was intended to be an outward expression of a deep, inward love for our creator God. Freddy Hayler's album and book are on the cutting edge of the era leading us back to true worship and holiness. Experience God's presence through this refreshing, new sound of God's prophetic voice in this new hour of 'Golden Alter' worship."

—Dick Reuben, Evangelist
Sound of the Shofar Ministries
Teacher and leader, Brownsville Revival

Are we sincerely hungry for a genuine visitation from God? Are we truly willing to pursue the Lord regardless of the cost? The music and message of Freddy Hayler help to issue a clarion call for this nation...to cry out to God in heartfelt repentance."

—Stephen L. Hill, Evangelist
Awake America Ministries

ANGELS IN PARADISE:

SHORES OF ETERNITY

WITH CD INSERT

ISBN-13: 978-0-88368-493-1
ISBN-10: 0-88368-493-4
Printed in the United States of America
© 2006 by Freddy Hayler

Whitaker House
1030 Hunt Valley Circle
New Kensington, PA 15068
www.whitakerhouse.com

Library of Congress Cataloging-in-Publication Data

Hayler, Freddy, 1955–
Angels in paradise : the shores of eternity / Fretty Hayler.
p. cm.
Summary: "Explores the mysteries and joys of heaven and shows what believers can look forward
to"—Provided by publisher.
ISBN-13: 978-0-88368-493-1 (hardcover with cd insert : alk. paper)
ISBN-10: 0-88368-493-4 (hardcover with cd insert : alk. paper) 1. Heaven—Christianity. I. Title.
BT846.3.H39 2006
236'.24--dc22   2006029069

1 2 3 4 5 6 7 8 9 10 11 ₩ 13 12 11 10 09 08 07 06

Contents

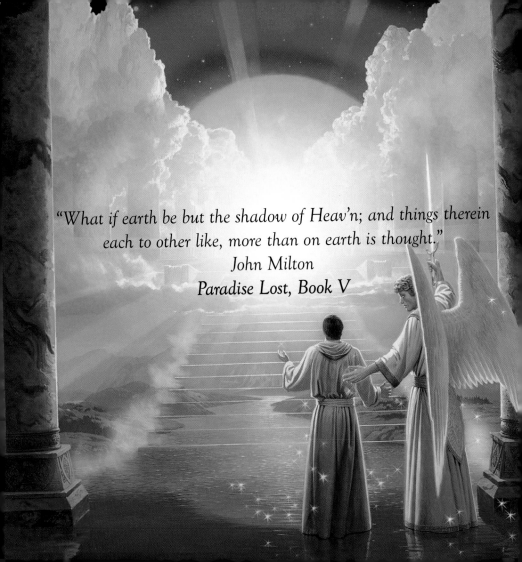

"What if earth be but the shadow of Heav'n; and things therein each to other like, more than on earth is thought."
John Milton
Paradise Lost, Book V

Your Final Destiny

Future in Paradise

All of us from time to time have imagined what heaven would be like. From TV specials to national televised series and even with the recent release of the movie Narnia, our generation has taken a great deal of interest in understanding more about heaven. A recent Gallup poll suggests that heaven is a topic of very high interest to both Christian and secular folk. What most people fail to realize is that, according to the Bible, heaven is more real and tangible than earth—more real than even our immediate surroundings.

About This Book

This book is not intended to be a doctrinal, theological tome regarding the doctrine of heaven. Rather, this book will thoroughly investigate certain clues already found in the Scriptures regarding the very nature and essence of paradise. The author has tried to make it clear whether or not a given topic is based on opinion or experiential testimony or whether it is clearly stated in the written Word of God. The music and lyrical accounts have been birthed out of a deep desire to teach the Word of God. In describing some of the attributes of paradise, sincere testimonies from godly saints from the past and present have also been utilized.

However, at Golden Altar Publishing, we are not interested in offering up our own concocted views on the doctrine of heaven, nor has it been our desire to simply push emotional buttons with information that is not supported by Scripture. Regarding the blessed doctrine of heaven, we have endeavored to maintain sound doctrine on the subject. Besides, our ability to perceive heavenly beauty is obviously limited while living in this realm. God has intended it to be so. This fact alone, however, has not deterred us from trying to make heaven as vivid a place as ever for the listener/reader.

With all the books about heaven circulating these days, I couldn't resist offering up one more biblical viewpoint on the subject and combining it with music and heavenly worship. Because the doctrine of heaven has been somewhat trivialized in certain cases lately, I felt it would be good to write a book that was more straightforward on the matter. It is also important that we don't try to make paradise something that the Bible does not represent it to be. However, we should not ever discount genuine testimonies from godly saints, past and present, who have given us their testimonies concerning paradise. This is especially true when their accounts do not contradict the Scripture. Certainly, it is not our goal to encourage Christians to live with their "heads in the clouds"; but the Bible clearly states it is quite natural for a believer to long for heaven.

For we know that if our earthly house of this tabernacle were dissolved, we have a building of God, an house not made with hands, eternal in the heavens. For in this we groan, earnestly desiring to be clothed upon with our house which is from heaven. (2 Corinthians 5:1–2)

It is true that God reveals Himself continually through everyday, ordinary things, and we can experience God's heavenly presence if we would but learn to appreciate Him in every little thing. However, there are times when God will cause us to ascend to the secret place of the Most High in our worship. When we begin to worship God with heavenly worship—worship that originates from heaven's throne—we will also receive great revelation of how magnificent and majestic God's heaven truly is. For all true revelation of God is birthed from a spirit of worship.

A Heavenly River

There is a river in paradise, a river of revelation and truth, a river of divine healing and glory, that is flowing into the church in this hour. Its fountainhead begins in paradise. However, this is a river that cannot be detected with the five senses. It is a heavenly river that can only be discerned by abiding in God's presence and worshipping Him more ardently than ever before. In the books of Ezekiel and Revelation, the Bible speaks of a heavenly river of glory that continually flows from beneath God's throne.

Jump On In!

It is time for all of us as believers to learn more about this heavenly river of glory and by a leap of faith jump in headfirst! No more ankle wading. And after jumping in, let us take the river to others who are in need so that they too may be touched and eternally changed.

May the Lord grant that we ascend in our worship to God and acknowledge His presence all the more so that we can see His glory revealed in new and marvelous ways.

As believers in this hour receive a heavenly vision, like Isaiah they will also be commissioned with a heavenly call to win the nations to Christ and to do the works of God among the peoples of the earth.

For our light affliction, which is but for a moment, worketh for us a far more exceeding and eternal weight of glory; while we look not at the things which are seen, but at the things which are not seen: for the things which are seen are temporal; but the things which are not seen are eternal. (2 Corinthians 4:17–18)

Introduction:
Paradise Found

God loves you. In these trying times, more than ever, God wants to show us all the love and goodness of His heart by giving us a glimpse of heaven. I love to sing of my risen Savior and tell of the glorious heaven where He dwells! I also love to sing about paradise and the love of God that will be there. *Angels in Paradise* explores the glory of the risen Christ and the beauty of God's heaven through worship, narrative, music, prophetic art, and Scriptures. It is our earnest prayer that, by getting a glimpse of the glory of the risen Christ and beautiful heaven where He dwells, you will be changed forever!

A *Paradise Perspective*

The apostle Paul was a man who kept one eye on heaven and one eye on earth at all times.

Paul said that he was caught up into heaven. He wrote to the Colossians the following Scriptures regarding the connection between your present status and having a scriptural understanding of where you are going. There are both practical and powerful implications when a believer firmly understands his heavenly destiny and calling.

> *We give thanks to God and the Father of our Lord Jesus Christ, praying always for you, since we heard of your faith in Christ Jesus, and of the love which ye have to all the saints, for the hope which is laid up for you in heaven, whereof ye heard before in the word of the truth of the gospel.*
>
> (Colossians 1:3–5)

You see, sometimes Christians seem surprised when they discover a great soulwinner like Paul made a connection between their heavenly hope and their earthly calling. It seems like understanding the truth about heaven also leads to a *livelier faith* in Christ on earth.

In the previous Scriptures, it is as if Paul was saying that there are already ordained

earthly works stored up in heaven if the earthbound believer can only see them. He said that your hope is already "laid up for you in heaven." And the hope he spoke of here is not just the future hope of heavenly bliss but of heavenly works to be accomplished by believers while living here on earth. One thing is sure, the visions of heaven and paradise that the Lord gave Paul definitely influenced his faith on earth.

It is not expedient for me doubtless to glory. I will come to visions and revelations of the Lord. I knew a man in Christ above fourteen years ago, (whether in the body, I cannot tell; or whether out of the body, I cannot tell: God knoweth;) such an one caught up to the third heaven. And I knew such a man, (whether in the body, or out of the body, I cannot tell: God knoweth;) how that he was caught up into paradise, and heard unspeakable words, which it is not lawful for a man to utter.
(2 Corinthians 12:1–4)

Certainly, the apostle Paul was no "flake." He was a great missionary and soulwinner who wrote two thirds of the New Testament!

A Newly Restored Eden

Everybody will die one day. Therefore, the most important thing you can do is to prepare for where you will spend eternity. And to all of you who are true believers in Christ, heaven is your final destination—your eternal home. It is wise for all of us to contemplate and learn a little more about heaven. After all, heaven will be around for all eternity!

Let's begin immediately to send our rewards ahead and to make earthly decisions with our heavenly destination in mind. And may we also endeavor through our witness to bring the atmosphere of heaven down to earth. For only the supernatural power of the Holy Spirit can effect beautiful change in the hearts of fallen man. It is vitally important that we learn to practice His heavenly presence continually and begin to worship and sing to the Lord with angelic passion while on earth. Jesus has given us a new song in these days and is preparing His bride to join with the angelic heavenly throng above in singing an anointed song of praise to Him. The poetry below is true.

He traineth thee for song,
For endless song above,
To lead heaven's burning seraph choirs
In ecstasies of love.

Let us join with the angels and heavenly hosts above in a new song of praise in paradise. Through simple faith in Jesus Christ, heaven is your destiny and paradise is found.

—Freddy Hayler

Part I–Garden in Paradise

"All about Heaven"

Chapter One
Heaven Is Above

In one sense, heaven is one infinitely large, grandiose garden. Some have even described it as a lush and beautiful planet! One thing is sure, it is an incredible place of abundance, fruitfulness, and prosperity. And God desires heaven to come down to earth in practical ways. His desire is to restore the Garden of Eden, which was lost through original sin.

Before original sin, Adam loved to tend the Lord's Edenic gardens. After his fall, he was consigned to hard labor by the sweat of his brow. Poverty, pain, anguish, and death became inevitable realities in his life outside the Garden. That's why Jesus became the Second Adam. His primary purpose is to save and restore health, prosperity, and eternal life to those who would accept Him as their Lord and Savior. Jesus, the Rose of Sharon, desires to restore all of us to pre-Adamic condition where once again

we can become faithful stewards of His Garden in Paradise.

The earthly glory of the first Eden will be eclipsed by the radiant glory of the new Eden that is soon coming to earth. Jesus, King of paradise, longs to give you and me a vision of the glories to come so that we will be all the more motivated to bring in the harvest that God has ordained for each of us to accomplish.

A Lofty Perspective

God has prepared for you and your loved ones a beautiful, pristine garden in paradise. The moment Adam and Eve fell from the Garden of Eden, God had an immediate plan to restore what was originally defiled by sin. For the garden in paradise is a garden that is untouched or unblemished by evil. The Scriptures seem to use the words *paradise* and *heaven* interchangeably. Some believe that the new earth will be heaven while others believe that heaven/paradise is above. Regardless of your position, it is certainly a glorious place!

God loves you. Let me say that again: God loves you. He truly does! In these trying times, more than ever, Jesus wants to show us all the love and goodness of His Father by giving us a glimpse of heaven. He wants us to have a taste of His wondrous works. He wants us to behold His beautiful countenance and His throne. He wants us to have a revelation of His goodness and kindness. Heaven is a *real place*. It is the place where God and His beautiful angels dwell—a literal destination for every believer. He wants you as His beloved people to know that He is the Prince of Peace and that everlasting peace and bliss is your final destination.

One day everyone will leave this world and will stand before God. Therefore, heaven is a very important topic for each of us to consider. As a matter of fact, it is one of the most important subjects that a believer should consider. One of the greatest missionaries who ever lived said, "In the final analysis, it is our conception of heaven and our perspective of life after death, which will answer every question life puts to us."

Yes, my friend, contemplating heaven is one of the most glorious things a Christian should do.

To Ascend

The Greek word for heaven is *ouranos*, which means "to ascend, to lift." This word is used some 272 times in the New Testament. "Heaven" must be a very important place to Jesus! The original classical Greek word for heaven is *baino*. It is the root word for *ouranos*. Similarly, it means "to go up" as in the sense of "to ascend up a large staircase." Early on in the Bible, the patriarch Jacob experienced this "going up" in a vision. He saw a stairwell descend from heaven.

And he dreamed, and behold a ladder set up on the earth, and the top of it reached to heaven: and behold the angels of God ascending and descending on it.

(Genesis 28:12)

Another meaning for the word *baino* is to "walk toward a destination, to mount up, to ascend."

17

Take an Extraordinary Journey

So consider, dear Christian, every day you live on this earth you are progressing toward an eternal destination. It would make sense for all of us to contemplate this wonderful place and destination. For the Bible always speaks of heaven as God's sphere—His own dwelling place. Could it be that God desires to reveal to this end-times' generation some of the glorious mysteries and treasures of paradise—*to open the very vault of heaven?*

Although the Bible does not go into great detail regarding heaven's actual design, there are still plenteous scriptural references from which we can deduce some truths regarding its nature.

If ye then be risen with Christ, seek those things which are above, where Christ sitteth on the right hand of God. Set your affection on things above, not on things on the earth. (Colossians 3:1-2)

Heaven is most often spoken of in Scriptures in relation to God's plan to save us through Christ—for Jesus longs to bring all of His people to heaven. The book of Revelation makes the most dramatic statements about heaven's scenery—its objects, its angels, its celestial beings, and the beauty and majesty of the post-Resurrection Christ. However, the important thing to remember here is that the Bible portrays heaven primarily in the sense that it is *God's place.* In the Lord's Prayer, Jesus refers to God as *"our Father which art in heaven"* (Matthew 6:9; see also Matthew 5:16, 45; 6:1), and Jesus Himself belongs to this realm.

In our endeavor to understand God's creation called "heaven," we claim no new doctrine or theology. But through music, visions, and spiritual impressions we hope to clarify and crystallize the Christian's concept of how truly glorious a place it is!

Let not your heart be troubled: ye believe in God, believe also in me. In my Father's house are many mansions: if it were not so, I would have told you. I go to prepare a place for you. And if I go and prepare a place for you, I will come again, and receive you unto myself; that where I am, there ye may be also. (John 14:1-3)

The Heavens Opened

Jesus said to His new convert, Nathanael,

Verily, verily, I say unto you, Hereafter ye shall see heaven open, and the angels of God ascending and descending upon the Son of man. (John 1:51)

So many of us are like Nathanael. We too would like to see the heavens opened. Many Christians often ask themselves questions such as, "What is heaven like? How will Jesus appear in heaven? What is the resurrected body like? What does the Bible say about heaven? How is paradise described in the Scriptures? What is its scenery and landscape? Does it have similarities with earth? What kind of celestial architecture exists there? Where is the Crystal Sea, and what is the throne of God like?"

It is true that the Bible is somewhat silent on some of these points of inquiry. However, there are also strong biblical references regarding aspects of heaven, such as the "garden of God" and heaven existing as an Edenic paradise.

Planet Heaven

Some Christians who have visited heaven (whether by a vision or with an angelic guide) claim that heaven is shaped like a sphere and appears earth-like. In virtually every account, it is seen as a place much larger and more grandiose than planet earth. The Bible does not speak of heaven as a celestial planet. However, it does speak about it as an actual, habitable place to live. And if it is, as Milton supposed in the intro quote to this book, more like earth than we think, it would seem logical to assume that it has at least some of the features of a friendly, habitable planet.

The Bible does speak about a perfect new creation where "the lion will lie down with the lamb." On numerous occasions, the Bible refers to the mountain of God, the Crystal Sea, fruitful trees, and beautiful surroundings that are quite similar to earth—only on a more grandiose scale.

Whether we use the word *planet* as a metaphor or not, it is still a beautiful description! However, the main goal of all that we have endeavored to do here is to explore our lovely God and Savior—the Lord Jesus Christ, the Fairest of Ten Thousand, the Rose of Sharon, and show some of the things that He has prepared for those who love Him. Certainly, all endeavors to adequately describe the reality of heaven must fall short since God and heaven exist in unimaginable glory and beauty.

But as it is written, Eye hath not seen, nor ear heard, neither have entered into the heart of man, the things which God hath prepared for them that love him. But God hath revealed them unto us by his Spirit. (1 Corinthians 2:9-10)

It is our prayer, then, that God reveals these unimaginable "things" to us in our journey. Keeping in mind that God Almighty Himself is the primary and cherished focal point of all our inquiry concerning heaven and the universe.

Folks will always ask questions, such as, "What happens after I leave this world?" "Where are my loved ones who have departed?" "What is heaven like?" "What does Jesus look like?" etc. This book will endeavor to explore these and many other questions regarding God and His abode.

Chapter Two
Heaven Is Real

Heaven Is a Locality

First of all, heaven has an actual *locality*. Its locality is described in the Bible quite simply as being "above."

Thou hast ascended on high, thou hast led captivity captive: thou hast received gifts for men.
(Psalm 68:18, emphasis added)

Wherefore he saith, When he ascended up on high, he led captivity captive, and gave gifts unto men. (Now that he ascended, what is it but that he also descended first into the lower parts of the earth? He that descended is the same also that ascended up far above all heavens, that he might fill all things.) (Ephesians 4:8–10)

O LORD our Lord, how excellent is thy name in all the earth! who hast set thy glory above the heavens. (Psalm 8:1)

It is in the divine plan to populate the third heaven above, where God dwells, which is also called "glory."

For it became him, for whom are all things, and by whom are all things, in bringing many sons unto glory, to make the captain of their salvation perfect through sufferings. (Hebrews 2:10)

After this I looked, and, behold, a door was opened in heaven: and the first voice which I heard was as it were of a trumpet talking with me; which said, Come up hither, and I will show thee things which must be hereafter. (Revelation 4:1)

The Lord invites the apostle John to come up hither. God desires us also to come up hither and to see His glorious dwelling place.

God has a very real address and resides in a very real and beautiful place called paradise. Heaven is the abode of God, the angels, the redeemed, and all the happy inhabitants of heaven! Heaven is not a state of mind. It is an actual and tangible place that God has created.

The LORD on high is mightier than the noise of many waters, yea, than the mighty waves of the sea. (Psalm 93:4)

But Jerusalem which is above is free, which is the mother of us all.
(Galatians 4:26)

Heaven Is a Place

Second, heaven is an actual *place*. It's a place where no one will ever have to say good-bye. Heaven is a place where Jesus will wipe away every tear from our eyes (if need be!). Heaven is a place where babies and children who have died before their time will be raised up and instructed by angels and will go on to live happily forever. Heaven is a place where the streets of the Holy City will be filled with children laughing and playing.

And the streets of the city shall be full of boys and girls playing in the streets thereof. (Zechariah 8:5)

The wolf also shall dwell with the lamb, and the leopard shall lie down with the kid; and the calf and the young lion and the fatling together; and a little child shall lead them. And the cow and the bear shall feed; their young ones shall lie down together: and the lion shall eat straw like the ox.
(Isaiah 11:6-7)

"Now I am going to return to my land, and I, myself, will live within Jerusalem. Then Jerusalem shall be called 'The Faithful City,' and 'The Holy Mountain,' and 'The Mountain of the Lord Almighty.'... and the streets will be filled with boys and girls at play." The Lord says, "This seems unbelievable to you–a remnant, small, discouraged as you are–but it is no great thing for me." (Zechariah 8:3, 5-6 TLB)

Heaven is a place where boys and girls play on streets of gold even as they frolic up and down the gently rolling, green hills of glory–where their sounds of laughter can be heard echoing over the fields and valleys of God's grand and glorious gardens! And as a child of God, God desires for you to be filled with wonder and childlike joy at the fact that one day soon, we'll all be children of the Father living in heaven with Him–forever.

That ye may be the children of your Father which is in heaven.

(Matthew 5:45)

Heaven is also a place of beauty and majesty. (See Revelation 21:1; Revelation 22:7.) Heaven is a place where kingdoms, princedoms, kings, thrones, dominions, angelic hosts, and generals of heaven from across the universe will flow unto God's throne in order to pay homage to the King of Kings and Lord of Lords.

Heaven is a *real place*. The apostle Paul was prohibited from revealing what he saw and heard in the third heaven of paradise. (See 2 Corinthians 12:1-9.) However, the apostle John was released and ordained by the Holy Spirit to vividly describe to the bride (the Lamb's wife!) many things regarding the beauty and majesty of the new earth and the new heaven.

Heaven is where Jesus, our glorified Lord and Savior, dwells. He is beautiful beyond compare! In Revelation 1:10-20, John also breathtakingly described for us

the glorious post-resurrection appearance of our Lord Jesus Christ.

A Tangible Place

Jesus also told us that heaven is a real and tangible place.

Let not your heart be troubled: ye believe in God, believe also in me. In my Father's house are many mansions: if it were not so, I would have told you. I go to prepare a place for you. (John 14:1-2)

Jesus said, "*If it were not so, I would not have told you.*" Jesus was not speaking metaphorically here. He is not playing with words or using analogies. In short, He is saying, "I'm not kidding around here. I'm not 'wordsmithing' here. This isn't a quip, a quote, or a slogan! I am not speaking to you in pretty symbolism. I am telling you *plainly* that heaven is a *literal* place where I am building you a *literal* mansion."

We know that heaven is an actual place because the Bible says that Jesus ascended into heaven—that is, He went from one *place* to *another*.

23

And no man hath ascended up to heaven, but he that came down from heaven, even the Son of man which is in heaven.

(John 3:13)

Jesus saith unto her, Touch me not; for I am not yet ascended to my Father: but go to my brethren, and say unto them, I ascend unto my Father, and your Father; and to my God, and your God.

(John 20:17)

And while they looked stedfastly toward heaven as he went up, behold, two men stood by them in white apparel; which also said, Ye men of Galilee, why stand ye gazing up into heaven? this same Jesus, which is taken up from you into heaven, shall so come in like manner as ye have seen him go into heaven. (Acts 1:10-11)

The Word of God specifically says that heaven is a place, for it specifically states that believers will be "within" it while unbelievers will be "without"—that is, they will be outside the "camp" or gates of heaven. Thus, heaven is not just a state of mind or something that dwells within

your heart or mind. No, it is so much more! It is an actual, physical place, existing in a spiritual plane in the universe.

Blessed are they that do his commandments, that they may have right to the tree of life, and may enter in through the gates into the city. For without are dogs, and sorcerers, and whoremongers, and murderers, and idolaters, and whosoever loveth and maketh a lie.

(Revelation 22:14-15)

Paradise—A Desired Haven

God has prepared for you amusements and activities that are beyond your wildest imagination. Heaven is a real place of unlimited joy and happiness where there is never any bad news but always good news. It's like visiting a favorite family vacation spot but the vacation doesn't end. There are trees and mountains, valleys, waterfalls, rivers, and oceans. Heaven is no bore. Heaven is fun and it will be fun for zillions of years without end into the future.

Heaven Is Full of Activities

Heaven is a dynamic and lovely place—it is full of adventure, and one will never tire of its activities and joys. If you want to know what heaven is like, just go and get a scenic calendar and think of that beautiful natural scene that God created on earth, only a hundred times more beautiful.

Heaven Is Full of Surprises!

The Father loves to surprise His children! In heaven there are many colorful festivities and social enjoyments. God likes to throw a good party. No, let me restate that. God likes to throw *extravagantly* good parties! Like God, we as earthly parents love to surprise our children—for example, at Christmastime or maybe a surprise birthday party. We love to "hide" our gifts from our loved ones and then, without warning, heap treasures upon them. We inherited this trait from our heavenly Father. As loving parents we would never surprise our children in a way that would cause them fear or confusion. So it is with the Lord. God is a loving, eternal Father who longs to surprise His children with all the pleasures of paradise.

Chapter Three
The Perfect Place

A Country beyond the Stars

God has put in the heart of every man, woman, and child a longing for eternal life and for a place where evil, sickness, disease, poverty, sin, and death do not exist. A poet correctly describes the state of the heart's eternal longing:

> My soul, there is a country far beyond the stars. For we all carry within us the eternal wonders we seek without us.

Long ago, the prophet King Solomon aptly made this observation:

> God has made everything beautiful for its own time. He has planted eternity in the human heart, but even so, people cannot see the whole scope of God's work from beginning to end.
>
> (Ecclesiastes 3:11 NLT)

All of us at times have wondered what heaven and eternity will be like—for God Himself has put eternity in our hearts.

The Transition Point

No believer needs to be overly concerned with his departure from this earth. The most beautiful entourage of angels will come and escort you into the presence of your loving Father, who loves you and is longing to see you and honor you. God has even used the tragedy of the fall of man in Eden as a means to secure the salvation of many through the Lord Jesus Christ. Since the fall, physical death has actually become the *divine transition point* for passing from the physical realm into the heavenly realm.

Although it was not God's original plan for man to die physically (He wanted Adam and Eve and their descendants to live forever in the Garden of Eden), Jesus Christ has now tasted death for every man, woman, and child—past, present, and future!

> But we see Jesus, who was made a little lower than the angels for the suffering of death, crowned with glory and honour; that he by the grace of God should taste

death for every man. (Hebrews 2:9)

In Psalm 23, the Lord tells us, His people, that He will be with us when we pass through the "shadow of death." This is because Jesus has tasted death for every believer already. The Good Shepherd is our transition point.

The LORD is my shepherd; I shall not want. He maketh me to lie down in green pastures: he leadeth me beside the still waters....Yea, though I walk through the valley of the shadow of death.
(Psalm 23:1-2, 4)

As hard as it is to see from our perspective at times, death is quite pleasant for a believer. For a believer who is born again, what the world calls "death" is only the beginning. Death is the primary vehicle of transportation to heaven for a believer. Death is a glorious transformation and process for a Christian.

As John Milton once said, "*Death is the great key that opens the palace of eternity.*" Because of man's fall in Eden, temporal pain and suffering is a reality in this fallen world. Still, no believer should be afraid to die, for death (or translation) is God's way of transporting His beloved into the joys of heaven.

And it came to pass, that the beggar died, and was carried by the angels into Abraham's bosom: the rich man also died, and was buried. (Luke 16:22)

And there shall be no more curse: but the throne of God and of the Lamb shall be in it; and his servants shall serve him.
(Revelation 22:3)

We must be mature enough as believers to see that, in this current age, the death of a believer is actually *progress*, for it is a transition point. In Christ, God has worked all things together for good and uses even death to move forward His plans and purposes. In Psalm 23, the Bible implies that a Christian will not fully experience death but will only see its "shadow." For death is not the end for a believer; rather, it is only a wonderful change and transformation.

Spiritual Metamorphosis

As a child I used to love to watch a moth or butterfly emerge from its cocoon with radiant and colorful glory. Like a lowly caterpillar's metamorphosis into a beautiful, colorful butterfly, so too all who have trusted in Christ for salvation will be changed for the better to the extreme! Some have even likened to saint's passing to the "birth canal" leading to eternity.

> *In a moment, in the twinkling of an eye, at the last trump: for the trumpet shall sound, and the dead shall be raised incorruptible, and we shall be changed.*
> (1 Corinthians 15:52)

> *Therefore if any man be in Christ, he is a new creature: old things are passed away; behold, all things are become new.*
> (2 Corinthians 5:17)

It has been said that only those who are ready to die are prepared to live for Christ on earth. This is true. In Acts 1:8, Jesus said that we are to be His "witnesses." In the original, *koine* Greek, the word *witnesses* means "martyrs." Therefore, unless you are willing to die for Christ, you are not really ready to live for Him, according to the Scripture.

Again, consider that, for a believer, death is the door to unlimited access to the presence of God as well as vast knowledge and wisdom.

> *For now we see through a glass, darkly; but then face to face: now I know in part; but then shall I know even as also I am known.* (1 Corinthians 13:12)

> *Beloved, now are we the sons of God, and it doth not yet appear what we shall be: but we know that, when he shall appear, we shall be like him; for we shall see him as he is. And every man that hath this hope in him purifieth himself, even as he is pure.* (1 John 3:2–3)

Brothers and sisters! Grieve not! There is great progress in the death of a believer!

> *They go from strength to strength, every one of them in Zion appeareth before God.* (Psalm 84:7)

And there shall be no more curse: but the throne of God and of the Lamb shall be in it; and his servants shall serve him: and they shall see his face; and his name shall be in their foreheads.

(Revelation 22:3–4)

Death will deal a "healing hand," for when a believer "flies" away from this world, he/she flies away from pain, rejection, sorrow, persecution, temptation, sin, oppression, evil surroundings, and the arrows of the enemy. In other words, departing this world is actually very beneficial for a true believer.

Precious in the sight of the LORD is the death of his saints. O LORD, truly I am thy servant; I am thy servant, and the son of thine handmaid: thou hast loosed my bonds.

(Psalm 116:15–16)

A good name is better than precious ointment; and the day of death than the day of one's birth. (Ecclesiastes 7:1)

The LORD is my shepherd; I shall not want. He maketh me to lie down in green pastures: he leadeth me beside the still waters. He restoreth my soul: he leadeth me in the paths of righteousness for his name's sake. Yea, though I walk through the valley of the shadow of death, I will fear no evil: for thou art with me; thy rod and thy staff they comfort me.

(Psalm 23:1–4)

God Is Not Spooky

Recent sci-fi movies have highlighted the theories that some astrophysicists have put forth and have glamorized, such things as worm holes, parallel universes, quantum/dimensional physics, folded universes, time/light travel, translation and string theory, etc. Others try to portray God as some *impersonal* energy force or make Him out to be some diffused spirit or some source of energy or light.

But God is a benevolent Creator—a loving and personal Savior to each person who would receive His Son as Savior. Folks tend to get blown away with the recent findings of science. They are stymied when they realize the sheer size and immensity of the universe. But God is foremost a personal God. He created time, space, gravity, light, and energy in order to make life possible on earth.

No Wasted Space

God created the forces and laws of physics of an entire universe for the purposes of making life possible on earth. One famous astrophysicist has stated that if this were the case, God has wasted a lot of space! But the fact is, this is not a "waste of space," as some have supposed. God's glorious creation of earth, the solar system, and the ever expanding universe has given everyone a clue to how caring, personal, and loving the Creator God of the universe truly is. I mean, He has really gone out of His way to make life possible on earth.

I think understanding His character also gives us a clue as to what heaven will be like. Obviously God is a God of detail and takes great care in His creation. Consider that there are over one trillion galaxies with over a hundred billion stars in each galaxy! However, there are only a limited amount of mid-sized yellow stars in each galaxy (those which are capable of sustaining life on a planet).

For example, a dwarf white star is far too small and too hot to support life in any given solar system, whereas a red giant (like Antares) is far too cool and too large. In addition, any solar system that can support life must be located near the mid-outer band of a spiral galaxy. This is because if it is too close to the center of the galaxy the cosmic rays and energy given off by the galaxy's nucleus (or black hole) would utterly make life impossible. Of course if it is too far from the center, it could be thrown off into interstellar space and would not benefit from the celestial tidal pulls of other stars and galaxies. Elliptical galaxies are not capable of supporting life, and these make up most of vthe galaxies in the universe. They are too diffused and dense in cosmic energy, and no biological life can exist within them.

In addition, a solar system located in a

spiral galaxy needs to have large exterior planets (such as Saturn and Jupiter) that act as celestial vacuum cleaners—attracting wayward asteroids and comets that have been jolted from the solar system's Ort cloud (the leftover fragments of the early solar system). Otherwise such wayward asteroids and meteorites would collide with the earth on a continual basis, making it impossible for life to exist on earth. There are many other aspects to a planet's size and location, as well as its make up, that determine whether or not it can support life. The fact is, there just aren't a lot of such planets or solar systems or even galaxies that exist in the entire universe.

God is quite organized and "together." He is not confused. He is the author of order, symmetry, and beauty. We see this on planet earth and also because of earth's unique position on one of the outer arms of our spiral Milky Way galaxy.

Vantage Points

God has foreordained our unique vantage point in the universe. He knew that one day many would be able to see an incredible display of His divine handiwork throughout creation. For example, from our vantage point on earth (depending on whether it's winter or summer) we can either look to the center of the galaxy and see certain constellations and nebulae, etc., or we can look out to the far reaches of interstellar space.

Backyard Astronomy

The book of Job describes the magnificent stars of Orion. Although we know that astrology is forbidden by the Bible (we know that God controls the stars and that mere starlight controls nobody's destiny!), God has set the constellations in their place as a testimony to the plan of redemption. In other words, the heavens tell a story visible to every person from his own backyard.

Of course God knew that one day there would be a Hubble space telescope. And although our ancient forefathers were only able to use their natural eyesight, there was still enough astronomical inspiration in their backyard view for them to confess the following. Although their field of view was much more limited than today, the heavens were still alive with the sound of music. The words of their song echoed forth the fact that God is a magnificent Creator of infinite power and design.

Then God brought Abram outside beneath the nighttime sky and told him, "Look up into the heavens and count the stars if you can. Your descendants will be like that—too many to count!"
(Genesis 15:5 TLB)

When I consider thy heavens, the work of thy fingers, the moon and the stars, which thou hast ordained; what is man, that thou art mindful of him? and the son of man, that thou visitest him? For thou hast made him a little lower than the angels, and hast crowned him with glory and honour.
(Psalm 8:3–5)

Because that which may be known of God is manifest in them; for God hath showed it unto them. For the invisible things of him from the creation of the world are clearly seen, being understood by the things that are made, even his eternal power and Godhead; so that they are without excuse.
(Romans 1:19–20)

The same complexity, beauty, and symmetry of creation that we see in the physical universe also exist in heaven—but to a much higher magnitude than we can conceive!

And he showed me a pure river of water of life, clear as crystal, proceeding out of the throne of God and of the Lamb. In the midst of the street of it, and on either side of the river, was there the tree of life, which bare twelve manner of fruits, and yielded her fruit every month: and the leaves of the tree were for the healing of the nations.
(Revelation 22:1–2)

Perfect Life

God is life. He is the vibrant source of all life. The closer you get to Him, the more "alive" you will become! Jesus came so that we as His people could live a more abundant life—not only in this life but also in the next!

> I am come that they might have life, and that they might have it more abundantly.
> (John 10:10)

And this abundant "eternity life" begins for a believer at salvation! (See John 3:2-4.) The abundant eternal life that Christ promises is already available to every born-again Christian on earth. However, in heaven this abundant life is totally perfected. In heaven, life comes to its full fruition—its ultimate pinnacle. Heaven is a place where no sin, defect, imperfection, confusion, temptation, or ungodliness is present. All the defects and imperfections that presently exist on this earth will not be present either in heaven or the new earth.

When the young, godly man named Stephen was passing from this world to the next, he saw a better country—a country even where Christ ruled from the right hand of the Father.

> But he, being full of the Holy Ghost, looked up stedfastly into heaven, and saw the glory of God, and Jesus standing on the right hand of God, and said, Behold, I see the heavens opened, and the Son of man standing on the right hand of God.
> (Acts 7:55-56)

The Grief Now Is Part of the Happiness Then

I'm sure that Stephen was gloriously surprised when Jesus stood to honor him as he was leaving this world. Wouldn't it be grand if Jesus would find each of us so faithful and true that when we pass from this life we would be so honored by Him that He would stand up from His throne as we entered?

"Narnia" Restored

All of us should understand this life on earth has an ultimate purpose in the economy of God. As a matter of fact, it appears that all the pains of life, the separation of loved ones, the trials and sufferings, even the occasional feelings of emptiness and loneliness, are all part of a master plan of the ages.

Could it be that the pain we experience now will be a part of the happiness then? Could it be that the pain of losing a loved one will be transformed into that much more of a blessing when we reunite with that loved one on heaven's eternal shores? Could it be that the sorrows now will be part of the joy then? Might such loss and senseless evil in life on earth increase the feelings of relief and joy that the old world is behind us even as the new world lies before us for all the ages to come? Could not all the pain and suffering be some sort of purification and even a source of joy and reward in paradise? We must see all from heaven's view and from God's eye! For God has worked *all things...together for good to them that love God, to them who are the called according to his purpose*" (Romans 8:28).

I'm also sure the repentant thief on the cross was joyously surprised when he was taken to paradise by Jesus and His angels. I'm sure there have been quite a few "street people" who have died believing in Christ who were just as surprised. I'm certain the poor, homeless beggars probably didn't expect a first-class, entourage of angels to show up to pick them off the streets and carry them to heaven!

And Jesus said unto him, Verily I say unto thee, To day shalt thou be with me in paradise. (Luke 23:43)

Thou wilt show me the path of life: in thy presence is fulness of joy; at thy right hand there are pleasures for evermore. (Psalm 16:11)

One thing is certain, Jesus, the lion of God, is coming on a white horse and will rescue the righteous from the forces of evil. For the Bible guarantees that in heaven Christ alone will be the only true Hero, the only true celebrity!

Heaven Is No Ghost Town

There are entire TV sitcoms now that inaccurately portray heaven and God's angels. Heaven is not a place where fat little infant-like cherubs float around on fluffy marshmallow clouds as some movies have portrayed. It's not a place for disembodied spirits or ghosts. Nor should God be portrayed as some vain, worldly, "out of it" comedian. The world has many misconceptions. Heaven is a glorious place—it is not a spacey or flaky place to write or sing about! Heaven is a biblical and very tangible reality—a very real physical and spiritual place in a dimension far greater than this. Heaven is where God lives. It is actually from this realm that all the other dimensions and realms of existence were created. And heaven is a perfect place!

Strange Concepts of Heaven

The devil loves to confuse folks, but the Bible says we are to have the mind of Christ. We should have the mind of Christ regarding what He has to say about heaven. I'm not against experiential testimonies of genuine saints who claim they have been to heaven, but the Bible is the only reliable source for verifying such claims. You see, my friend, it is an actual place, of course—a glorious and wonderful creation that God created for the enjoyment of Himself, the angels, the redeemed, and all the happy inhabitants of heaven! The enemy has tried to use ignorance and outright strange imagination to make heaven appear to people on earth as boring or even "spooky."

Devilish Imagery

The devil constantly tries to make it appear like something that it's not. We've all heard of analogies such as "heaven is in your head" or "heaven is nothing but the spirit world." From the medieval frescos painted on the vaulted ceilings and rotundas of historic cathedrals to contemporary art, we are constantly reminded of the folly of such infantile concepts of paradise. Sadly, "heaven" has been primarily promoted by ignorant artists, secular philosophers, and poets.

Wimpy Angels?

There are a lot of misconceptions about heaven and its creatures. For example, from fiction books and New Age thought to current prime time TV series and movies, all too often angels are portrayed as weak, overly silly, effeminate, and infantile creatures. It is because of false mentalities such as this that unlearned folk go around saying things such as this: "Heaven is a place where you just float around on clouds and play harps with other fat little infant cherubs who possess rosy cheeks and who are either naked or scarcely clothed!"

How utterly ridiculous! The devil constantly makes heaven try to appear weird. He loves to create misconceptions in the human imagination and in the mind. (See 2 Corinthians 10:3-5.)

Planet Paradise

Although heaven is very similar to earth, it has been created in a different and higher dimension and on a much more perfect and grandiose scale than planet earth. The devil does not want you to know these things! After all, God created the earth as the original Paradise for mankind to live in. It is only because of original sin that the law of sin and death took hold. Even the laws of physics and other laws of the created universe have been stained and disrupted. Sadly, the post-Edenic earth is but a distant reflection of what once was the perfect Garden of Eden.

So he drove out the man; and he placed at the east of the garden of Eden Cherubims, and a flaming sword which turned every way, to keep the way of the tree of life.

(Genesis 3:24)

Thank God that He had a plan to send His Son, Jesus. Even before the foundation of the world, He could foresee how things would play out in human history. His plan is to recreate heaven and earth into a *perfect place* where the spirit of love, joy, righteousness, and peace will reign!

[Jesus] *the heaven must receive until the*

*times of restitution of all things, which
God hath spoken by the mouth of all his
holy prophets since the world began.*

(Acts 3:21)

Heaven Is a "Familiar" Place

As Milton supposed, why wouldn't heaven be a life-supporting planet much like our own terrestrial earth? Milton and others have always believed that heaven could very well be a much more familiar place, like Earth, than we imagine.

I say that heaven is a familiar place because God loves His creation. He loves His mountains and His valleys. He loves His trees, plants, and flowers. He is quite fond of His rivers, His oceans, and all the fish and creatures that live within them. As we've already seen, God also loves His animal creations. And, of course, He adores you and me! Why would we think for a moment that He would drastically change His taste and preferences in creating paradise? Why do some think that everything there will be in the form of a disembodied spirit? That's not consistent with God's character at all!

The Lord has said that He has prepared a "literal" mansion for us. Jesus, our heavenly carpenter (or our heavenly stonecutter!) has beautifully crafted a custom home for each of us! When He says to us that we will have a personal residence in the New Jerusalem, He means it!

Heaven is not filled with disembodied spiritual substance. Your spirit man is not a "puff of smoke." Also, God should not be conceived as some diffused spirit or impersonal energy source of the universe.

And heaven is not to be described as simply a tunnel of light or a series of wormholes that lead to other realities. God has created a real and tangible physical place where all of his children are destined to live one day. He has created a familiar place for the enjoyment of His people, His angels, and, of course, for Himself!

Spirit Matter

Speaking of real and tangible heavenly

substance, when my wife, Anne, encountered an angel several years ago, she noticed that his heavenly body was more beautiful, real, and alive than her own physical body! His face was so beautiful and lovely. The brassy and brilliant substance of his skin was indescribable and his eyes were large, beautiful, and compassionate—like dove eyes. Yet, his physical frame was so strong that she could tell he could have destroyed an entire city in the blink of an eye.

The fact is that there are no earthly words and there is no earthly painting that could come close to describing this angel. In terms of beauty, strength, power, holiness, and purity, he is indescribable! (As far as his composition and form, he was very brilliant.) He looked and acted like a familiar friend, although he appeared somewhat stymied—almost quizzical in his expression as if he was asking himself as to why on earth God Almighty was so interested in someone born of woman and made of fallen human flesh. He also seemed very excited to exit the house in order to ascend back to the presence of the Father.

Heavenly Substances

Yes, the substances in heaven are more real, tangible, and touchable than the physical matter that is on earth—regardless of its form or density. I'm so glad that God created the physical universe, and I am especially overjoyed that He also created a real place called heaven. Again, I say it will not be an unfamiliar place because God takes great care in designing His creation. In the Bible, God speaks of His love for the mountains, trees, valleys, plants, flowers, rivers, fish, and animals that He created for our enjoyment. Obviously He loves the earth, for He created it. Why would we think He would change His taste so drastically in creating heaven?

Again, the Lord wants His people to know that when He speaks of mansions in John 14, He meant literal mansions. He was not speaking metaphorically. The things of heaven are much more perfect and grandiose than anything we can experience on earth. Heaven is a very real and tangible place. One could think of it as a perfect existence—a paradise where no evil or sin has ever sullied or maligned. Your loved one who died while believing in Jesus Christ is now in a wonderful place—a place of great joy and life. A place of adventure in the glory of God!

The Spiritual "Physics" of Celestial Perfection

Yes, my friend, heaven is a beautiful and real place just like the earth but much larger and more perfect. For the sting of original sin has never touched its blissful environment. God loves you and loves the physical things He has created, and He has a definite plan of restoration. And He is about to conquer the final enemy, which is physical death!

And God shall wipe away all tears from their eyes; and there shall be no more death, neither sorrow, nor crying, neither shall there be any more pain: for the former things are passed away.

(Revelation 21:4)

The Celestial Broadway

The apostle John told us of a literal highway that runs through the middle of the Crystal City. On either side of it, God has planted lavish vegetation and lush fruit trees that adorn its riverbanks.

And he showed me a pure river of water of life, clear as crystal, proceeding out of the throne of God and of the Lamb. In the midst of the street of it, and on either side of the river, was there the tree of life, which bare twelve manner of fruits, and yielded her fruit every month: and the leaves of the tree were for the healing of the nations. (Revelation 22:1–2)

The Language of Heaven

To those who are not born again or who are not filled with the Spirit, all of this talk of glory may appear cryptic or unclear. But to the spiritually minded (when proper principles of biblical interpretation are applied), the Bible is very clear in its language. Unlike man, God is not in any way deceptive or illusive—especially with language. Unlike false preachers, He does not attempt to change the meaning of words. He does not twist truth to meet an objective that has ulterior motives or hidden agendas. There is no deception in God.

Language and the meaning of words are important to God. He does not play tricks with words, nor does He try to deceive the mind. In short, God speaks plainly. God's language is precise and mathematical. As God is unchangeable, so are His words. His truth is straightforward, logical, and concise.God's language and truth have never evolved, nor will they evolve, for there is nothing *new* under the sun. What folks call "new truth" is really nothing but truth *rediscovered*. The fact is the Bible is clear that heaven is glorious and that heaven is a perfect and tangible place.

The simple truth is that heaven is a very real and glorious place made similar to earth. However, objects in heaven will be different from objects on earth, only to the extent that they are more perfect and grandiose and that they have the unique ability to reflect God's glory and light. I guess you might say they are "translucent" in that they allow for some light to pass through them. As we have said before, one could think of it as an incredibly large, lush, greenish-blue planet teeming with life and gently suspended in the celestial heavens like a large, radiant living jewel.

The Greatest Hope

My friend, this is a real and perfect existence—a lush paradise that no sin or evil has even sullied or maligned. Child of God, if you have lost a loved one who had genuine faith in Christ, rejoice in the fact that his precious soul now abides in a beautiful and wonderful place—a place of great joy and life! For heaven is a place of ceaseless, creative adventures and the glory of God! The sting of original sin has never touched its blissful environment, nor can it ever.

Yes, heaven will be a familiar place for God's people. God loves you, and He loves the natural things that He has created. He has a definite plan of restitution for this old earth. He will not allow His glorious creation to be stained much longer by the scourge of the traitor cherub. For if one day with the Lord is as a thousand years, this means that Satan attempted to disrupt creation only six celestial days ago! Are we not living in the seventh day of God's creation? Is not the number seven His number for completion? The time of restoration is sooner than you think!

Creation's Clues

The intricate creation of our planet earth and its ecosystem, the universe, and the human body are clear proof that a personal and loving God exists. Such beauty and organization is proof that He is the grand master of all design and architecture in the natural universe. And if the natural universe is so beautiful, what must heaven look like?

Because that which may be known of God is manifest in them; for God hath showed it unto them. For the invisible things of him from the creation of the world are clearly seen, being understood by the things that are made, even his eternal power and Godhead; so that they are without excuse. (Romans 1:19-20)

When I consider thy heavens, the work of thy fingers, the moon and the stars, which thou hast ordained; what is man, that thou art mindful of him? and the son of man, that thou visitest him? For thou hast made him a little lower than the angels, and hast crowned him with glory and honour. (Psalm 8:3-5)

Against Vain Philosophy

The Bible warns us not to pay attention to humanist scholarship or the vain philosophies and concepts of men regarding God, life, reality, and death.

Beware lest any man spoil you through philosophy and vain deceit, after the

tradition of men, after the rudiments of the world, and not after Christ.

(Colossians 2:8)

From Plato to Lucretius, from Kant to modern existentialists and nihilists, the world's thinkers have miserably failed in explaining what is truth. As Christians, we know who is Truth, and that settles it. (See John 14:6.)

I am the way, the truth, and the life: no man cometh unto the Father, but by me.

(John 14:6)

And ye shall know the truth, and the truth shall make you free. (John 8:32)

You diligently study the Scriptures because you think that by them you possess eternal life. These are the Scriptures that testify about me. (John 5:39 NIV)

Scientists, physicists, and secular philosophers with their theories, metaphysics, and epistemologies in the end have virtually given us no clue as to who God is, who we are, and where heaven is or what it will be like. The false religious crowd fares no better.

Since the time of ancient Babylon, religious thinkers have been demonically inspired to conceive of heaven in a countless variety of strange ways. One only needs to read the Egyptian book of the Dead, the book of the Vedas, the writings of Buddha, or the Koran to see that they offer no clear understanding of life after death.

For we have not followed cunningly devised fables, when we made known unto you the power and coming of our Lord Jesus Christ, but were eyewitnesses of his majesty. (2 Peter 1:16)

Neither give heed to fables and endless genealogies, which minister questions, rather than godly edifying which is in faith: so do. (1 Timothy 1:4)

Only the Bible offers mankind a comprehensive and clear view of what heaven and hell are like. Only Christianity has an in-depth revelation of eternal life. The fountain of all knowledge and wisdom, Jesus Christ, has come to us and has given us a crystal clear understanding of salvation and the heavenly realm.

Speaking about Jesus, the apostle Paul said, *"In whom are hid all the treasures of wisdom and knowledge"* (Colossians 2:3).

Insulting!

I remember the story of the pseudo-intellectual evolutionist who walked down a beach one day and found an intricately designed, beautiful, gold, Swiss-made watch. He thought to himself, "Evidently, over millions of years, this surf and sand arbitrarily and by chance molded this watch." God is insulted by such reasoning—not to mention the Swiss watchmaker!

Now how can any logical or rational creature of God propose that non-thinking atoms—be they sand, primordial soup, or water molecules (even over trillions of years of time)—could by chance auto-assemble into a living, thinking, self-conscious creation of such sophistication, complexity, beauty, and design. Preposterous! Ludicrous! So many today insult their Creator God, who has created living things that are far more complicated than any gold, Swiss-made watch.

Cosmical Design

It is edifying to survey the cosmical design, the very fingerprint of God that is interwoven in the fabric of the universe. My family and I enjoy astronomy for this reason. For in the creative universe, we see the symbol of God's omnipotence, wisdom, and infinity. In creation, we see God's teleology and intelligent design. It is true that man can take inanimate substances and artfully create something of beauty from something God has already created. God is a Creator, but man can only rearrange. Paradise is an incredibly well-designed place—it is because it was designed by God Himself.

In God's natural creation, His objects are organized and animated by living principles that are innate. They are fashioned from within and bloom with life outwardly. As a matter of fact, beholding infinity in space gives us a clear concept of our own finite nature and our need to be dependent upon God for everything! That's why I feel the anointing every time I point my reflector telescope at the multitude of deep space objects that He has created. The heavens truly declare the glory of God! For the night sky with its starry constellations is the most awesome gospel tract ever written! Again, if the second heaven is this glorious, what must the third heaven be like?

A Familiar Cosmology

Again, it bears repeating that the beauty of nature and the world around us give us a hint that heaven will not be a totally unfamiliar place. This is especially true to those who know Christ and love to hear His voice while living here on earth. In the "sweet hour of prayer," God's elect will have already learned to hear His voice and to feel His sweet presence. How can heaven be an unfamiliar place to one who loves prayer and who knows the Master's voice? For Jesus, our Lord, will be there! And haven't we grown so accustomed to hearing His still, small voice by faithfully praying to Him while on earth?

In addition, our friendly guardian angels who have monitored and protected our lives since childhood will be there to greet us as well. For when we get to heaven we shall realize how many times Jesus had dispatched them to "carry us through" many a trial and tribulation.

Take heed that ye despise not one of these little ones; for I say unto you, that in heaven their angels do always behold the face of my Father which is in heaven.

(Matthew 18:10)

Our saved loved ones and friends will be there. All the great saints will be there. Most of all, Jesus, the "Bright and Morning Star" waits for us there!

Heavenscapes

Heaven's landscape will also be somewhat familiar, for it is glorious to behold and even more beautiful than the most breathtaking views of our terrestrial planet earth. Even the following children's song should give us a concept of heaven's beauty since this prayer acknowledges the earth's beauty as a precursor to heaven's beauty. The earth is a tangible manifestation of God's artistic sense of beauty. It testifies that "indeed God makes all things well." It is no wonder that anyone should imagine heaven as so glorious! You see, we can learn something about how beautiful heaven is by simply looking at creation and reading the words to the children's tune below.

All things bright and beautiful,
All creatures great and small,
All things wise and wonderful,
The Lord God made them all.

Each little flower that opens,
Each little bird that sings,
He made their glowing colors,
He made their tiny wings.

The purple-headed mountain,
The river running by,
The sunset and the morning
That brightens up the sky.

The cold wind in the winter,
The pleasant summer sun,
The ripe fruits in the garden,
He made them every one.

He gave us eyes to see them,
And lips that we might tell,
How great is God Almighty,
Who has made all things well.
                               – C. F. Alexander

During autumn, when my family and I have had the opportunity to drive through the multicolored Appalachian mountains of North Carolina, our childlike wonder of God and His creation is renewed. Even adults would do well to contemplate the truths illustrated in the above poetry. We should ever lose our childlike wonder when it comes to contemplating God's marvelous creation and the heaven wherein He dwells. We must never forget to trust entirely in Him.

Verily I say unto you, Except ye be converted, and become as little children,

MARVELOUS

ye shall not enter into the kingdom of heaven. (Matthew 18:3)

Forever Young

We should never allow the mysteries and enigmas of life on this earth to ever cause us to lose our childlike excitement regarding paradise. Remember, our perspective in this sphere of reality is somewhat limited by our vantage point on earth—that is, unless we become childlike in faith and soar into the heavenlies through prayer! Yes, we must be like little children so that we also may "see the kingdom of heaven." As a trusting little child who looks up to his earthly father, we should also have the same trust and teachableness toward our heavenly Father.

Fresh Perspectives

When God by His Spirit gives us a vision or a new perspective of heaven, it is like an earthly father taking his child out on a clear summer night to look at the stars. Or it's like a husband walking with his wife along a quiet beach or walking through the woods and talking about the wonders of God's created, physical world. By simply observing God's physical creation, we will be totally awed and overwhelmed with joy by the beauty of the world God has given us. Why would we think that God would not show us heaven in the same way? In fact, God desires to take our hands and walk each of us through the Word of God. He yearns to show us by His Spirit that heaven is a very real and beautiful place—His own garden in paradise.

Beautiful Earth—God's Footstool

Some of you may have recalled reciting the above-referenced poem as children. Such beauty of God's creation naturally leads us to conclude that heaven, His abode, is even more beautiful and glorious. For God Himself calls the earth His "footstool."

Thus saith the LORD, The heaven is my throne, and the earth is my footstool: where is the house that ye build unto me?

and where is the place of my rest?
                    (Isaiah 66:1)

But if God's "*footstool*" is so beautiful and majestic, what must His throne look like? And if His throne is more beautiful than the earth, what must His private chambers look like?

In summary, heaven is a place where *there will be eternal life in its fullness.* (See Matthew 25:46; Romans 2:7; 1 Timothy 4:8.) It is a place where there will be *eternal rest* and *peace.* (See 2 Corinthians 4:17.) It is a place of *unlimited knowledge.* (See 1 Corinthians 13:8–10.) It is a place of unmitigated *holiness* and *perfection.* (See Revelation 21:2.) It is a place of *joyful duty* and service to the Lord. (See Revelation 22:3.) It is a place of *pure worship.* (See Revelation 19:1.) It is a place of *social fellowship.* (See Hebrews 12:23.) It is a place of unfettered *communion with God.* (See Revelation 21:3.) It is a place of *extreme beauty.* (See Revelation 21:1–22:7.) There are degrees of *bliss* and *rewards* in this glorious place as well. (See Daniel 12:3; 2 Corinthians 9:6.)

In "Seventh Heaven"

Some believe that paradise, or heaven, is a reality that is subdivided into different dimensions of glory, gradations or levels of bliss. In 1 Corinthians 12, the apostle Paul spoke of a "*third heaven.*" Some believe that when Paul spoke of the third heaven, he was referring to the place that is solely the abode of God, and they teach that the *first heaven* is only the physical earth's atmospheric heaven. (See Job 26:11; Psalm 78:23; Isaiah 2:18; Daniel 7:13.)

Which also said, Ye men of Galilee, why stand ye gazing up into heaven? this same Jesus, which is taken up from you into heaven, shall so come in like manner as ye have seen him go into heaven.

(Acts 1:11)

However, in the Scriptures, when Paul implied that there is a *second* heaven, he was referring to our natural solar system or what scientists call "outer space," the reality of time, space, and dimension where the physical universe exists. (See Genesis 1:1–2.)

That in blessing I will bless thee, and in multiplying I will multiply thy seed as the stars of the heaven. (Genesis 22:17)

And lest thou lift up thine eyes unto heaven, and when thou seest the sun, and the moon, and the stars, even all the host of heaven, shouldest be driven to worship them, and serve them, which the LORD thy God hath divided unto all nations under the whole heaven.

(Deuteronomy 4:19)

Immediately after the tribulation of those days shall the sun be darkened, and the moon shall not give her light, and the stars shall fall from heaven, and the powers of the heavens shall be shaken.

(Matthew 24:29)

The third heaven (where God Himself lives) must be the place that Paul was referring to.

I was caught up into the third heaven fourteen years ago. Whether my body was there or just my spirit, I don't know; only God knows. But I do know that I was caught up into paradise and heard things so astounding that they cannot be told.

(2 Corinthians 12:2–4 NLT)

For Christ has entered into heaven itself to appear now before God as our Advocate. He did not go into the earthly place of worship, for that was merely a copy of the real Temple in heaven.

(Hebrews 9:24 NLT)

After this manner therefore pray ye: Our Father which art in heaven, hallowed be thy name. Thy kingdom come. Thy will be done in earth, as it is in heaven.

(Matthew 6:9–10)

Take heed that ye despise not one of these little ones; for I say unto you, that in heaven their angels do always behold the face of my Father which is in heaven.

(Matthew 18:10)

I am the living bread which came down from heaven. (John 6:51)

And hearken thou to the supplication of thy servant, and of thy people Israel, when they shall pray toward this place: and hear thou in heaven thy dwelling place:

and when thou hearest, forgive.
(1 Kings 8:30)

The LORD is in his holy temple, the LORD's throne is in heaven: his eyes behold, his eyelids try, the children of men.
(Psalm 11:4)

Return, we beseech thee, O God of hosts: look down from heaven, and behold, and visit this vine. (Psalm 80:14)

Thus the third heaven is the highest heaven, where the Father's "private chambers" exist. This dimension of existence is far above and beyond the very sphere (astrophysicists now believe that our entire universe is in the shape of a sphere) of the physical universe with its billions of galaxies.

A Hubble's-Eye View

Recently, NASA's Hubble space telescope has indicated that there are some twelve billion galaxies in the known universe. Floating 580 kilometers above the earth, the Hubble space telescope is now capturing views of the universe with greater clarity than ever before. The new advanced camera for surveys and a revived near-infrared camera and multi-objects spectrometer have already produced the most glorious set of images imaginable! Mankind for the first time is seeing directly the infinity of God's creation.

When I Survey

When I consider thy heavens, the work of thy fingers, the moon and the stars, which thou hast ordained. (Psalm 8:3)

Remember, God strategically placed our own planet earth on the outward ban or outer spiral of the Milky Way so we could see the glories of His created universe. Since we now know that there are billions of galaxies and millions of solar systems in those galaxies and hundreds of billions of stars, God is obviously not at all concerned about *space* in heaven's realms. It is estimated by some genealogists that over twelve billion people have lived on planet earth since the time of Adam and Eve. However, God's creation is so vast that there has been at least one galaxy created by God for each soul who has ever been born on the earth—plenty of room for everyone! And as vast as the universe is, God's abode is greater still!

"Cream" Always Rises to the Top

To the general assembly and church of the firstborn, which are written in heaven, and to God the Judge of all, and to the spirits of just men made perfect.
(Hebrews 12:23)

God's saints who have surrendered to the utmost to do His will, and who have allowed God to work within them Christlikeness; those who have surrendered to the Spirit and have allowed Him to work within them a Spirit-formed, stainless character, and as a result have done great works in His name; who have maintained their integrity, fidelity, purity, and honor, will find themselves "rising to the top" in paradise.

Every man's work shall be made manifest: for the day shall declare it, because it shall be revealed by fire; and the fire shall try every man's work of what sort it is.
(1 Corinthians 3:13)

Rejoice, and be exceeding glad: for great is your reward in heaven: for so persecuted they the prophets which were before you.
(Matthew 5:12)

What rewards in heaven does Jesus speak of? Spiritually speaking then, God always wants you and me to live in the "top of the tower." Again, this depends on how one has lived for Christ on this earth. The more you live for Him here, the closer you will dwell with Him on the level where His luxurious chambers exist!

Chapter Four
Beautiful Visions

Beatific Visions

You don't necessarily have to die in order to see Jesus and the glorious heavens wherein He dwells. You see, there is this condition of the heart called *purity* that is required before excellent spiritual eyesight can be acquired. It was Jesus Himself who said that only a "few" would be saved.

> *Because strait is the gate, and narrow is the way, which leadeth unto life, and few there be that find it.* (Matthew 7:14)

> *So the last shall be first, and the first last: for many be called, but few chosen.*
> (Matthew 20:16)

He also said that the pure in heart will "see" God. (See Matthew 5:8.) Who are the pure in heart? Those who have been washed in the blood of the Lamb and who have overcome the evil one.

The time is short, my friend. It's time for us to be totally honest with God. It's time to stop fooling yourself. Are you living pure before God? If you are prayerful and looking upward enough, God may grant you a vision of the heavenly city even as He granted Abel, Enoch, Noah, Abraham, and Sarah.

> *By faith Abraham, when he was called to go out into a place which he should after receive for an inheritance, obeyed; and he went out, not knowing whither he went....For he looked for a city which hath foundations, whose builder and maker is God....But now they desire a better country, that is, an heavenly: wherefore God is not ashamed to be called their God: for he hath prepared for them a city.*
> (Hebrews 11:8, 10, 16)

God has created a very tangible and celestial city for the happy inhabitants of His kingdom *"whose builder and maker is God"* (Hebrews 11:10). In Revelation 21, the apostle John was given a beautiful vision of how this "better country" is constructed and arrayed. Through the Spirit, the apostle Peter could also clearly see that

God will create a new heaven and a new earth. (See 2 Peter 3:13.)

Could that age be upon us? If we would be willing to receive beatific visions of heaven and of God, we, too, would experience a fresh vision of God in the glorious face of Jesus Christ, even as other Christians throughout the ages have experienced. And this would be an inconceivably ravishing vision that would change us forever! A beatific vision will change you and me even as it did Peter, James, and John. John became as a "dead man" and was slain in the Spirit in response to the visage of Christ's heavenly glory in the first chapter of Revelation.

His head and his hair were white like wool, as white as snow. And his eyes were bright like flames of fire. His feet were as bright as bronze refined in a furnace, and his voice thundered like mighty ocean waves. He held seven stars in his right hand, and a sharp two-edged sword came from his mouth. And his face was as bright as the sun in all its brilliance. When I saw him, I fell at his feet as dead. But he laid his right hand on me and said, "Don't be afraid! I am the First and the Last."

(Revelation 1:14–17 NLT)

Can you imagine what the Roman soldiers must have felt like by seeing just one of God's angels roll away the stone?

And, behold, there was a great earthquake: for the angel of the Lord descended from heaven, and came and rolled back the stone from the door, and sat upon it. His countenance was like lightning, and his raiment white as snow: and for fear of him the keepers did shake, and became as dead men.   (Matthew 28:2–4)

Hopefully, some of these soldiers got enough fear of the Lord to get saved!

Just consider how such beautiful, heavenly visions may have impacted the prophets as well, as the disciples of old. The following scriptural accounts are breathtaking to say the least.

Six days later, Jesus took Peter, James, and his brother John and led them up a high mountain by themselves. His appearance was changed in front of them, his face shone like the sun, and his clothes became as white as light....When the disciples heard this, they fell on their faces and were terrified. But Jesus came up to them and touched them, saying, "Get up, and stop being afraid."

(Matthew 17:1-2, 6-7 ISV)

The appearance of the wheels and their work was like unto the colour of a beryl: and they four had one likeness: and their appearance and their work was as it were

a wheel in the middle of a wheel....And above the firmament that was over their heads was the likeness of a throne, as the appearance of a sapphire stone: and upon the likeness of the throne was the likeness as the appearance of a man above upon it. And I saw as the colour of amber, as the appearance of fire round about within it, from the appearance of his loins even upward, and from the appearance of his loins even downward, I saw as it were the appearance of fire, and it had brightness round about. As the appearance of the bow that is in the cloud in the day of rain, so was the appearance of the brightness round about. This was the appearance of the likeness of the glory of the LORD. And when I saw it, I fell upon my face, and I heard a voice of one that spake....When they stood, these stood; and when they were lifted up, these lifted up themselves also: for the spirit of the living creature was in them....And the cherubims lifted up their wings, and mounted up from the earth in my sight: when they went out, the wheels also were beside them, and every one stood at the door of the east gate of the

LORD's house; and the glory of the God of Israel was over them above.

(Ezekiel 1:16, 26–28; 10:17, 19)

Higher Expectations

Don't think for a minute that their spiritual faculties weren't illuminated and enlarged by such encounters. Just because most Christians have never had such extensive prophetic visions in the past, that doesn't preclude them from experiencing them in the future. *Never* limit a supernatural God by unbelief, skepticism, or *low expectation*.

However, Bible prophecy is the final canonized perspective of God on all matters of faith and belief. All of us are blessed and our hearts are enlarged whenever we read the books of the prophets or when we read John's vision in the book of Revelation.

I beheld till the thrones were cast down, and the Ancient of days did sit, whose garment was white as snow, and the hair of his head like the pure wool: his throne was like the fiery flame, and his wheels as burning fire. A fiery stream issued and came forth from before him: thousand thousands ministered unto him, and ten thousand times ten thousand stood before him: the judgment was set, and the books were opened. (Daniel 7:9–10)

All of us need to contemplate the beautiful visions of glory described there more frequently. Yes, my friend, heaven is a very real place, and a vision of heaven and of Jesus will change your life forever!

Blessed is he that readeth, and they that hear the words of this prophecy.

(Revelation 1:3)

The "Lion and the Lamb"

We on earth need a vision of heaven—where all is at peace and where the wolf and the lion lie down with the sheep. The earth needs heaven's peace more than ever. Consider that the only chapters in the Bible where war and violence are nonexistent are the first two chapters of the Bible and the last two chapters of the Bible. (See Genesis 1–2 and Revelation 21–22.) The first state of total peace in the world was in the first Garden of Eden. The second and final state of peace in the world will come when the garden of paradise has been fully restored upon the new earth at the second coming of Christ.

Until the garden of paradise comes down to earth, there will be no peace among men or nations; there will be no peace in the entire creation (including the animal kingdom!) until Jesus Christ, the Prince of Peace, rules and reigns in the restored garden of Eden—the new heaven and the new earth!

And it shall come to pass in the last days, that the mountain of the Lord's house shall be established in the top of the mountains, and shall be exalted above the hills; and all nations shall flow unto it. And many people shall go and say, Come ye, and let us go up to the mountain of the LORD, to the house of the God of Jacob; and he will teach us of his ways, and we will walk in his paths: for out of Zion shall go forth the law, and the word of the LORD from Jerusalem. And he shall judge among the nations, and shall rebuke many people: and they shall beat their swords into plowshares, and their spears into pruninghooks: nation shall not lift up sword against nation, neither shall they learn war any more. (Isaiah 2:2–4)

Regardless of its noble attempts, the U.N. will never bring peace to this world. Only if the hearts of men are changed by the redeeming power of the blood of Jesus can there be peace on earth. As Corrie ten Boom said, "Men live together as brothers, only in the kingdom of our Lord—nowhere else."

If the leaders of the U.N. cannot cause the lion to lie down with the lamb, how will they ever be able to calm the vengeful, hateful, violent, greedy, lustful hearts of wicked mankind? In Jeremiah 17:9 the Scriptures say that hell, wickedness, and deception are bound up in the heart of man. Both man and beast have the potential for violence and destruction because since the fall these things have been bound up in their hearts.

But the Bible speaks of a time when the lion will lie down with the lamb.

> The wolf also shall dwell with the lamb, and the leopard shall lie down with the kid; and the calf and the young lion and the fatling together; and a little child shall lead them. And the cow and the bear shall feed; their young ones shall lie down together: and the lion shall eat straw like the ox. (Isaiah 11:6–7)

God's Animal Kingdom

The Prince of Peace Himself shall dwell among His creation and will tame them with the rod of the spirit of peace. God loves animals and is sorrowful over the violent and mean spirit that entered creation through the fall of Lucifer and the sin of man.

> And God created great whales, and every living creature that moveth, which the waters brought forth abundantly, after their kind, and every winged fowl after his kind:

and God saw that it was good. And God blessed them, saying, Be fruitful, and multiply, and fill the waters in the seas, and let fowl multiply in the earth. And the evening and the morning were the fifth day. And God said, Let the earth bring forth the living creature after his kind, cattle, and creeping thing, and beast of the earth after his kind: and it was so. And God made the beast of the earth after his kind, and cattle after their kind, and every thing that creepeth upon the earth after his kind: and God saw that it was good. (Genesis 1:21–25)

All was "good"—including the animals and pets of Adam and Eve. Then Lucifer convinced Adam and his wife, Eve, to sin and conspire against God. But I am glad that God was merciful. For when mankind backslid to the great degree to which they did, He didn't shut the whole thing down!

> And God saw that the wickedness of man was great in the earth, and that every imagination of the thoughts of his heart was only evil continually. And it repented

the LORD that he had made man on the earth, and it grieved him at his heart. And the LORD said, I will destroy man whom I have created from the face of the earth; both man, and beast, and the creeping thing, and the fowls of the air; for it repenteth me that I have made them. But Noah found grace in the eyes of the LORD.

(Genesis 6:5–8)

He found one righteous man named Noah. He also loved His animal creation so much and desired to preserve that investment on an ark. Noah and his family were good folks and became good stewards of quite a few pets themselves!

We are not robots. Adam chose to sin against God, while Noah chose to obey God. God saw potential and entrusted Noah with a righteous seed and with all of His wonderful animals. I'm so glad that God also gave me a free will that would allow me to freely choose to love Him.

The Practicality of Vision

And it shall come to pass afterward, that I will pour out my spirit upon all flesh; and your sons and your daughters shall prophesy, your old men shall dream dreams, your young men shall see visions. (Joel 2:28)

You see, visions from heaven can have a very practical effect on our lives. Noah received a vision from heaven that warned him to prepare for the preservation of his family while he lived on earth. He provided for his family both provision and shelter for the tough times that were coming.

We need to learn from Noah's life. Jesus said we would live in the same kind of wicked generation that Noah and his family lived in. All of us should spiritually "keep our ear to the ground" so that we might hear God's warnings in this hour.

One of the ways God will communicate to us is through visions and dreams. Being open to visions and dreams from the Lord is an additional change we need to make to our prayer lives in this hour. When was the last time you received a beatific vision or dream from the Lord? The Bible says you are to have the mind of Christ. God has given each of us a beautiful mind with the ability to receive anointed imaginations and visions from His Spirit. He *"is no respecter of persons"* (Acts 10:34). When we surrender such divinely created faculties to the Holy Spirit, God is able to grant us beautiful visions of Him and show us His will.

There was an ordinary man in the book of Acts named Cornelius. He was very devout. The Bible says he prayed to God continually.

> *He saw in a vision evidently about the ninth hour of the day an angel of God coming in to him, and saying unto him, Cornelius. And when he looked on him, he was afraid, and said, What is it, Lord? And he said unto him, Thy prayers and thine alms are come up for a memorial before God.* (Acts 10:3-4)

Are you willing to receive an angelic visitation or beatific vision? Would you be willing to receive a spiritual impression of heaven from the Holy Spirit if God were to give it? Do you look heavenward like Cornelius and continue in prayer daily? Do you help the poor? A "Cornelius-like" Christian will always be simultaneously both heavenly minded and earthly minded; thus he can accomplish much earthly good.

Chapter Five
The Homecoming

A Family Affair

There are loving bonds that will surpass even the grave! On this earth, there are family ties and strong bonds that are eternal. I have heard many ask the question, "Will Christians in my immediate family be with me in heaven? Will I meet my ancestors there?" I do not believe that familial ties and relationships among our family members will end in death. As the old hymn goes, "May the circle be unbroken." There is truth in those words. God created the family unit—it was His idea from the beginning. He ordained the first family in the Garden of Eden. Families consist of fathers, mothers, children and grandchildren, cousins, aunts and uncles, etc. Secular sociologists call the basic social unit of parents and children "the nuclear family." However, in the Bible the word *family* can be used in a wider sense.

You are the children of those prophets, and you are included in the covenant God promised to your ancestors. For God said to Abraham, "Through your descendants all the families on earth will be blessed."
(Acts 3:25 NLT)

It is true that in one sense all of God's children are forever now part of the larger family of God. All believers are now "related" to each other through the royal blood of Jesus Christ. Because of this fact, we are all considered by Christ to be "blood" brothers and sisters.

For this cause I bow my knees unto the Father of our Lord Jesus Christ, of whom the whole family in heaven and earth is named. (Ephesians 3:14-15)

God is interested in preserving the unique familial relationships that exist and that have been preordained by Him. The song *Garden in Paradise* vividly describes, through a vision, the excitement of parents and family members as they reunite in heaven. There is great shouting, leaping, and jumping for joy upon the recognition of family members. Some of these family members may have died prematurely or in an accident, but in heaven they are in a state of beauty and perfection.

Reunion beyond the Stars

Some may question this, but the Bible is clear that family members on earth who die in Christ will reunite with their Lord and with one another in heaven. Take, for example, the untimely death of King David's son. When David's child died prematurely, David prayed and fasted, and God comforted him by the Spirit by revealing to him that the child was in Abraham's bosom—paradise.

> And he said, While the child was yet alive, I fasted and wept: for I said, Who can tell whether GOD will be gracious to me, that the child may live? But now he is dead, wherefore should I fast? can I bring him back again? I shall go to him, but he shall not return to me.

(2 Samuel 12:22–23)

King David was saying, "I cannot bring him back from the dead. I love this child and one day I will pass through the shadow of the valley of death and will go to him in Abraham's bosom. I can go to him, but he cannot come to me. Therefore, I should live holy and love God so that I can go to where my son is." This is why, in Psalm 23:6, David could write that he had found peace in understanding that he would spend eternity in heaven with God and that he would see his infant son again. We, like David, need to know that God will keep our loved ones intact and has a plan to keep their lives preserved forever!

A Glorious "Homecoming"

As I said, families are important to God. For instance, every fifty years during the Jubilee celebration, the Israelites were told to return to their own natural families. Family reunions are important on earth and will continue to be in heaven. God believes in family reunions on earth and in heaven! He values our close relationships and preordained them.

> And ye shall hallow the fiftieth year, and

> *proclaim liberty throughout all the land unto all the inhabitants thereof: it shall be a jubilee unto you; and ye shall return every man unto his possession, and ye shall return every man unto his family.*
>
> (Leviticus 25:10)

When God gave the Abrahamic covenant, He didn't say to Abraham that He would bless the "individuals" of the world but that, through him, He would bless the "families" of the world. At that time in history, there were not many families on the earth. God was not just speaking of families in the sense of the *ta ethne*, people groups or nations, but He was speaking more particularly about a "tribe," a family related by genes, or what we would call blood relatives.

> *And I will bless them that bless thee, and curse him that curseth thee: and in thee shall all families of the earth be blessed.*
>
> (Genesis 12:3)

> *So concerning them Moses commanded Eleazar the priest, and Joshua the son of Nun, and the chief fathers of the tribes of the children of Israel.* (Numbers 32:28)

God sees redemption not only in terms of the individual, but also in terms of the entire family. In the New Testament, the Greek word for family is *oikos*, meaning, "a dwelling, a house or a household family."

> *They replied, "Believe on the Lord Jesus and you will be saved, along with your entire household."* (Acts 16:31 NLT)

Family ties and family responsibility are high priorities with God and always will be.

> *But if she has children or grandchildren, their first responsibility is to show godliness at home and repay their parents by taking care of them. This is something that pleases God very much.*
>
> (1 Timothy 5:4 NLT)

In 1 Corinthians 1:11 and 16:15, the apostle Paul honored certain families and their households. God will also continue to honor families and their relationships in heaven.

Although the Bible is not totally clear on this subject, it is my personal belief that the Scriptures strongly infer that family members may even dwell near each other in glory. Certain believers who have actually been caught up into heaven have testified that there will be villages of entire families who will ascend the Mount of God together to worship. These family members will not be idle, but they will be engaged in the employments and enjoyments of heaven. They will be involved in joyful service. For no one in heaven is ever bored or idle. Godly families will stroll the lush, green-carpeted hills of heaven, praising God and enjoying conversation with their brethren from other families as well. What a beautiful sight it will be to see Christian families together once again, full of unmitigated joy, with happy faces beaming.

Although all of us will be married to Jesus Christ, the Lord will still acknowledge and bless our close family relationships from earth. It is only that the joy of those relationships will be perfected in His love. And in the heavenly home there will be no strife, no bickering or arguing—ever again!

You may still ask, "Will my mansion and your mansion be located near other family members' homes in heaven?" I think it's a strong possibility that they will!

Chapter Six
A New Garden

Restoring the Garden in Paradise

Thankfully, God has a plan to restore the eternal bliss of paradise. With original sin came sickness, disease, poverty, evil, calamity, accidents, and death.

In the sweat of thy face shalt thou eat bread, till thou return unto the ground; for out of it wast thou taken: for dust thou art, and unto dust shalt thou return.
(Genesis 3:19)

Since the fall of Adam and Eve in the Garden of Eden, no man or woman has ever had the ability to control the foreordained day of their departure. God makes no mistakes—He kindly allows the correct amount of time for each of us to live on earth so that we can do our best at the seat of judgment.

There is no man that hath power over the spirit to retain the spirit; neither hath he power in the day of death.
(Ecclesiastes 8:8)

Because God foresees that a soul has reached its maximum eternal potential for reward, out of mercy, He takes some before their time. Also, many times God will take a righteous soul early because He sees an evil day that is coming and wants to spare that precious soul any undue pain.

The righteous perisheth, and no man layeth it to heart: and merciful men are taken away, none considering that the righteous is taken away from the evil to come. He shall enter into peace: they shall rest in their beds, each one walking in his uprightness. (Isaiah 57:1-2)

Since the fall of man, God has predestined and chosen for each believer a glorious date to leave this physical world. There was a great general who once taught his soldiers to face the battle knowing that their lives were in God's hands. He taught them not to be concerned with the fixed date that God had ordained for their homecoming. None of us should be fearful of the day that God has already fixed for our departure. "To think like this," the general said, "was to live a brave and courageous life"—on the battlefield or off.

Eternal Boomerangs

The Aussies enjoy throwing a U-shaped object made of wood called a boomerang. A good boomerang thrower can always cause the boomerang to return to himself. God is a very good "boomerang thrower." His elect will always return to Him and as just spirits who were made perfect because of their obedience to Christ in this life. Every baby born into this realm is an eternal spirit that has been created by God and for God. As they are exposed to truth on earth they have some decisions to make that will determine whether they will return to God.

Babies in Heaven

Now I'm not saying that God is an Australian, although there seem to be a lot of His people living in that country these days! But it seems to me (through the gift of childbirth) that He "flings" thousands of souls out of eternity every day only to have them hopefully return to Him once more. Those who have been aborted have a special blessing since those children will be raised in heaven by angels! However, the unrepentant ones who have willfully perpetrated this crime against these innocents will not go unpunished.

Their feet rush into sin; they are swift to shed innocent blood. Their thoughts are evil thoughts; ruin and destruction mark their ways. (Isaiah 59:7 NIV)

Remember, the only ones who will not return to His garden in paradise will be the ones who willfully chose not to because they loved evil and sin more than they loved righteousness and truth.

Eat from This Tree

Jesus is a tree of life for anyone who would partake of His supper. Yet there is an actual tree in heaven from which streams forth eternal life. In the garden of Eden, the Tree of Life continually bore fruit that would cause one to live forever. Many would like to return there but they do not know the way. The primitive yearning remains unfulfilled.

The image of God (mankind) was severely marred by Adam and Eve's passion for sin. Yet, since the time of Eden, God has set eternity in every human heart.

God has made everything beautiful for its own time. He has planted eternity in the human heart, but even so, people cannot see the whole scope of God's work from beginning to end.

(Ecclesiastes 3:11 NLT)

All of us would like to live forever. But in man's unredeemed evil state, human hearts possess a propensity for evil where their wickedness would only be infinitely multiplied if given the chance.

And God saw that the wickedness of man was great in the earth, and that every imagination of the thoughts of his heart was only evil continually. And it repented the LORD that he had made man on the earth, and it grieved him at his heart. And the LORD said, I will destroy man whom I have created from the face of the earth. (Genesis 6:5-7)

Holy Limitations

God has wisely put a brake on unrestrained evil. Imagine an evil earthly tyrant having the ability to live forever and being able to project his evil acts against other people without limitation. To solve this dilemma, God allowed for physical death. God is very efficient. He curtailed evil upon the earth.

Eternal Prisons

God created hell as a sort of eternal prison for dark souls who choose to love evil. Even fallen human governments construct prisons to endeavor to separate violent and wicked criminals in order to protect the innocent. God is also merciful and will spare the peace and joy of heaven from being destroyed by evildoers. Besides, hell is a place where evil hearts will be able to practice wickedness upon each other without limitation.

There Is a Fount

I always hear people ask me what happened to the people who were born before Christ.

> But unto every one of us is given grace according to the measure of the gift of Christ. Wherefore he saith, When he ascended up on high, he led captivity captive, and gave gifts unto men. (Now that he ascended, what is it but that he also descended first into the lower parts of the earth? He that descended is the same also that ascended up far above all heavens, that he might fill all things.)
> (Ephesians 4:7-10)

You see, God had a marvelous plan. He sent His Son as a sacrifice for all those who came before Him and who would come after Him. He even went to those souls who died in past history—prior to His coming—and rescued them and brought them to heaven. For He will redeem all who choose Christ as their salvation. And through the power of the Holy Spirit of grace, He will conform them to the image of His own dear Son, thus recreating the image of Christ in these second Adams. But the second Adams will be more perfect (*the imago dei*)—for they will be fit to dwell in heaven forever.

> For in the image of God made he man.
> (Genesis 9:6)

God has always desired to restore man to the image of Himself!

Father Knows Best

Did you know that the time of each soul's departure is based upon the wisdom and mercy of God? As I said earlier, it is based upon what God sees to be the best possible outcome for a Christian in eternity. It is also based upon how far along the potential process is regarding the image of Christ being realized in that person.

The Divine Gardener

You see, *God will pick a flower in full bloom*, for He knows each person's future and how best they will be able to perform before His august and holy judgment seat. God is so merciful. We must begin to see things from His perspective.

Death was not God's initial idea for man, but in the Garden of Eden, man willfully chose sin and has been doing so ever since. God did not create robots. Let's face it, because of the treachery of Lucifer and the fall of a third of the angels, sin and evil had already reared their ugly heads in heaven, and God was not unaware that the fallen archangel would also eventually try to destroy His highest creation through temptation and sin. (See Job 1; Isaiah 14; Ezekiel 28.)

I believe God would have taught Adam about sin, evil, and temptation, but it was a whole different ball game when Adam and Eve willfully committed treason against God and personally allied with Satan (what they in fact did was directly rebel against God Almighty). Again, they chose to *personally experience evil* and make it a part of their *nature.*

You see, Adam and Eve's appetite desired evil. They would not be content to be instructed by God in how to hate and avoid evil. Adam and Eve passionately felt they must "sow their wild oats." They felt they must *ingest* evil and experience sin firsthand. And ever since, mankind has suffered from the evil desire of the lust of the eyes, the lust of the flesh, and the pride of life.

For all that is in the world, the lust of the flesh, and the lust of the eyes, and the pride of life, is not of the Father, but is of the world. (1 John 2:16)

After all, the Lord warned them not to eat from the Tree of Knowledge of Good and Evil. And being godlike in their free will, He would not prevent them.

And the LORD God said, Behold, the man is become as one of us, to know good and evil: and now, lest he put forth his hand, and take also of the tree of life, and eat, and live for ever....So he drove out the man; and he placed at the east of the garden of Eden Cherubims, and a flaming sword

71

which turned every way, to keep the way of the tree of life. (Genesis 3:22, 24)

Premature death was not His idea either. God originally ordained for all of His creation to live forever, but because Adam sinned this brought physical death for all of his descendants. It was actually God's mercy that He placed two mighty cherubim with flaming swords to guard the Tree of Life, for if Adam had eaten from that tree of eternal life, he would have been *locked* into spiritual death forever.

Mankind became "Cainish" and murderous. However, there were some (like Abel) who through conscience listened to God's "still small voice" and through the things created could believe in a holy God and see the need for sacrifice and atonement for their sins. Abel, Enoch, Noah, and Abraham could prophetically see their need for Christ—even though most people during their generations loved wickedness.

In other words, it was actually God's *mercy* that prevented man from living forever!

Because of the wickedness that man willfully desired by eating from the Tree of Knowledge of Good and Evil, mankind had the potential to do unlimited evil, and God could foresee the outcome.

And the Lord said, My spirit shall not always strive with man, for that he also is flesh: yet his days shall be an hundred and twenty years. (Genesis 6:3)

Thus, God has limited our earthly life spans out of mercy. In this current *aion* (the Greek word for age) of history, the Father is very wise to have shortened man's ability to live on earth to a maximum of approximately 120 years—and it is not because He desires anyone to die. As unpleasant as physical death may seem from this side of eternity, it is actually a manifestation of God's mercy.

Heavenly Midwives

Remember, dear saints, death should be seen by the believer as a veritable "birth canal" into eternity, with the Holy Spirit and His angels being heavenly midwives.

For a believer, death is the passageway to heavenly glory and ecstasy forever.

You have made known to me the path of life; you will fill me with joy in your presence, with eternal pleasures at your right hand. (Psalm 16:11 NIV)

In regard to a Christian's time of leaving this world, physical death was God's method of stopping spiritual death—thus freeing the Christian to become eternally righteous like the faithful angels and to live in a glorious realm that evil cannot touch. God never wanted His creation to be eternally separated from Him in a state of spiritual death. At the same time, He did not want to create loveless and lifeless automatons or unfeeling robots either! No, He wanted to deal with the problem of evil by sending His only Son, the Lord Jesus Christ, to die for the sins of men. Jesus would taste death for each and every one of us.

And you hath he quickened, who were dead in trespasses and sins.

(Ephesians 2:1)

He willingly shares His glory with those who willingly choose Him. No doubt, by eating from the Tree of Life, Adam and Eve would have suffered a far more unpleasant and devastating death—even eternal death!

So the LORD God banished him from the Garden of Eden to work the ground from which he had been taken. After he drove the man out, he placed on the east side of the Garden of Eden cherubim and a flaming sword flashing back and forth to guard the way to the tree of life.

(Genesis 3:23-24 NIV)

God could have ended the whole history of man right there in the Garden. But instead, He allowed Adam and Eve to conceive and bear children. He had an ultimate plan of redemption in mind in order that man might become Christlike and thus partake of the Tree of Life that is in heaven!

Chapter Seven
The "Mirage" Becomes a Pool

Sometimes life is complicated, and everyday trials and circumstances can make the promise of heaven appear like a mirage on a distant horizon. But one day soon, the journey of life on this earth will be over and the thirsty, desert traveler will find an abundant pool of living water.

> And the burning sand and the mirage shall become a pool, and the thirsty ground springs of water. (Isaiah 35:7 AMP)

All believers one day will depart this world for eternity. The question at hand is, What will your final destination be like as a Christian? Specifically, what else does the Bible say about paradise? The prophet Isaiah conveyed to us the fact that our faith, hope, and all our aspirations as believers will very soon become reality. The promise of heaven will become a concrete reality one day soon. Heaven is no "state of mind" but is a real place. The "mirage" will become a real, tangible pool of water.

The vision of heaven God has put in your heart will soon become a reality. And do not discount the possibility that not only will you see your loved ones there, but the Lord Jesus may also surprise them with visits with biblical heroes like David or Samson!

This one thing is certain—heaven is a real place. Let me restate for a moment what the Bible is clear on in regard to what heaven will be like:

- In *heaven*, there is eternal life. (Matthew 25:46)

- In *heaven*, there is real glory. (2 Corinthians 4:17)

- In *heaven*, there is ever growing knowledge. (1 Corinthians 13:9–10; 1 John 3:2–3)

- In *heaven*, there is rest. (Hebrews 4:9)

- In *heaven*, there is pure, undefiled holiness. (Revelation 21:27)

- In *heaven*, there is creative work and holy service to the Lord of Hosts. (Revelation 22:3)

- In *heaven*, there is pure worship. (Revelation 19:1)

- In *heaven*, there is royal society, conversation, and communion with God, and with the redeemed brethren. (Revelation 21:3)

In any event, we must preach heaven more than ever if we are going to experience a true revival on earth. Life must seem like a "mirage" to those who do not have a heavenly perspective. Christians must know that all their hopes and aspirations will become a reality. By knowing this, they will have more confidence in serving God while here on earth. Like the apostle Paul, they must know that, even if they die, *"to live is Christ, and to die is gain"* (Philippians 1:21).

That's why Paul was so daring in his efforts to win souls and to plant churches—

he knew that even if he was martyred it was a win-win situation.

Do you have daring faith? If you say no, then I will pray for you to get a vision of paradise!

It is not expedient for me doubtless to glory. I will come to visions and revelations of the Lord. (2 Corinthians 12:1)

You see, Paul was a heavenly-minded missionary who feared no one but God. Persecution and martyrdom were no big deal to him. Death was no problem for him either, for he kept before him the vision of paradise.

For to me to live is Christ, and to die is gain....For I am in a strait betwixt two, having a desire to depart, and to be with Christ; which is far better.
(Philippians 1:21, 23)

Paul had heavenly revelation. He knew that since the fall of Adam what the world sees as "physical death" is only a spiritual translation to paradise. In other words, prior to either the rapture or the second coming of Christ, death is the primary vehicle that translates believers into glory. A glorious and beautiful entourage of the angels of God will transport every believer right into God's presence!

> And it came to pass, that the beggar died, and was carried by the angels into Abraham's bosom: the rich man also died, and was buried. (Luke 16:22)

No Earthly Good?

God has one Son, and He was a missionary. No one was a greater earthly missionary than Jesus. He went to the worst of sinners and did not remove Himself even from the worst cases of human need. Yet Jesus needed a heavenly perspective to endure the suffering and shame of the cross.

> Looking unto Jesus the author and finisher of our faith; who for the joy [glory] that was set before him endured the cross, despising the shame, and is set down at the right hand of the throne of God.
> (Hebrews 12:2)

It is important that believers keep one eye on heaven and one eye on earth while they sojourn. A famous Scottish preacher was once asked if he was looking forward to heaven. He replied, "What are you talking about, man? I'm in heaven right now." In other words, like Abraham, this brother had his eyes fixed on a better country constructed with better substances.

> But now they desire a better country, that is, an heavenly: wherefore God is not ashamed to be called their God: for he hath prepared for them a city.
> (Hebrews 11:16)

There needs to be more preaching on the doctrine of heaven in our churches. The preaching and imparting of a vision of heaven for centuries has given great hope to those who literally have nothing in this life. The poor, the elderly, the infirm, and the unlearned must not only be taught about their authority in Christ and how to prosper in this world, but they also need to be taught the blessed hope of heaven. For such a vision of heaven is a great anchor to the soul.

Like all great reformers, Wesley preached a lot about heaven, and, during the Industrial Revolution, his homeland in England was spared the bloody uprising of the impatient, unrestrained, impetuous masses that France experienced. So then, preaching about heaven to the generation living on earth at this time will help to impart necessary patience and hope to those who seem as though they are without hope. Of course it's better to teach a man to fish than to give him a fish—it's better to show heaven in practical ways than to simply talk about it. That's what great reformers did then and do now. Wesley set up provision for food, clothing, and education (especially religious) for the colliers and coal mining families of England. He planted a cell group in virtually every borough in England and allowed the Word of God to prosper among even the poorest people.

Again, preaching about heaven to those in this world will impart a spirit of patience. This is not a cop-out. It seems as if nowadays everyone is so competitive and ambitious that they want to get their "heaven" on this earth. But our forefathers were wiser in this and liberally preached about heaven. They loved the old hymns about glory and heaven and the "by-and-by." In fact, the doctrine of heaven has practical, beneficial psychological and social ramifications as well. The preaching of the doctrine of heaven leads to stability in the soul. It is the reason why so many soldiers with a righteous cause could march right into death with total peace. They had a heavenly perspective.

You see, my friend, if Lazarus did not possess in his heart a heavenly perspective; if he thought there was no heaven; if he believed that there was no paradise—no Abraham's bosom—he may have ransacked the rich man's house and thrown the inhabitants out!

And there was a certain beggar named Lazarus, which was laid at his gate, full of sores....And it came to pass, that the beggar died, and was carried by the angels into Abraham's bosom: the rich man also died, and was buried....But Abraham said, Son, remember that thou in thy lifetime receivedst thy good things, and likewise Lazarus evil things: but now he is comforted, and thou art tormented.

(Luke 16:20, 22, 25)

The Heavenly Shepherd

The Lord is our earthly and heavenly Shepherd, and He will guide us into green pastures—greener than any pastures you could ever imagine!

The LORD is my shepherd; I shall not want. He makes me to lie down in green pastures; He leads me beside the still waters....Surely goodness and mercy shall follow me all the days of my life; and I will dwell in the house of the LORD forever.

(Psalm 23:1–2, 6 NKJV)

When a person we know and love who is a believer passes on, we should not "want." For a Christian there is a short-lived grief that is good. It's okay to emotionally miss the earthly presence of a loved one. But, we should not be overly concerned or anxious about where a believer has departed to and where they now abide. Heaven is a glorious and beautiful place beyond compare! The apostle Paul, who had visited paradise himself, had this to say to a group of grieving believers at Thessalonica:

But I would not have you to be ignorant, brethren, concerning them which are asleep, that ye sorrow not, even as others which have no hope. For if we believe that Jesus died and rose again, even so them also which sleep in Jesus will God bring with him. (1 Thessalonians 4:13–14)

79

Chapter Eight
A Heavenly Form

A Glorious Body

All bodies in heaven will be fully restored and youthful, being beautiful to look upon.

> For we know that if our earthly house of this tabernacle were dissolved, we have a building of God, an house not made with hands, eternal in the heavens. For in this we groan, earnestly desiring to be clothed upon with our house which is from heaven. (2 Corinthians 5:1-2)

The devil hates anything that's taken from the Bible as *literal*. He is an anti-literalist! He loves weird and spacey metaphors. He laughs at loopy and flakey notions of "planet" heaven. He is a liar and he always is trying to make the Scriptures seem non-literal and untruthful. He contradicts common sense. The devil hates the literal, resurrected body of Christ. That's why there are so many strange ideas circulating around regarding the resurrected body and the tangible image of Christ. If the Bible says that after His resurrection He appeared as a man, then He appeared as a glorious man. It's that simple. Consider that Jesus in His glorified form is said in the Bible to have a glorious, resurrected body that is very similar to the body He had on earth. The Scriptures speak of both the pre-incarnate Christ and the resurrected Christ as having man-like (anthropological) forms and features.

> And they saw the God of Israel: and there was under his feet as it were a paved work of a sapphire stone, and as it were the body of heaven in his clearness....And the sight of the glory of the LORD was like devouring fire on the top of the mount in the eyes of the children of Israel. (Exodus 24:10, 17)

> His head and his hairs were white like wool, as white as snow; and his eyes were as a flame of fire; and his feet like unto fine brass, as if they burned in a furnace; and his voice as the sound of many waters. (Revelation 1:14-15)

Imago Dei

The redeemed are created in His image. The human soul is meant to reflect the divine image. However, the human soul in a sinful state cannot properly reflect the image of God since it has been distorted by sin. Unless a soul has been redeemed, it cannot fully reflect the "imago Dei," the image of God. Only a soul washed in the blood of Jesus and born again by the Spirit of God can fully reflect the image of God that was marred after the fall. The unsaved soul cannot reflect the pure image of God. God resurrects and preserves the redeemed's body so that He can rejoice in the very image of His own dear Son reflected in His people—His precious, spotless bride.

Our resurrection as believers will not be just a "spiritual" one, but our bodies will also rise again in a newly perfected constitution of heavenly substance.

But God giveth it a body as it hath pleased him, and to every seed his own body.... There are also celestial bodies, and bodies terrestrial: but the glory of the celestial is one, and the glory of the terrestrial is another....So also is the resurrection of the dead. It is sown in corruption; it is raised in incorruption: it is sown in dishonour; it is raised in glory: it is sown in weakness; it is raised in power: it is sown a natural body; it is raised a spiritual body. There is a natural body, and there is a spiritual body.

(1 Corinthians 15:38, 40, 42-44)

The countenance and features of the redeemed are glorified, handsome, beautiful, comely, and radiant. In heaven, a believer's condition, his state of mind, his intellectual faculties, his moral character, and even his appearance will be perfected. In other words, your condition will be gloriously improved for the greatest good possible. Your senses, mind, and faculties will be enlarged in Christ. Every believer will not only receive an endless life but will also receive life in all its *fullness!*

Like the Stars Above

Astronomers tell us that in the entire

universe, there do not appear to be any two stars that are exactly alike. Each star is different in its size, color, and hues. The Bible likens the uniqueness of each resurrected believer to "stars." Out of all the happy inhabitants of heaven, your star will shine uniquely in its brilliance, color, and hue.

> *And they that be wise shall shine as the brightness of the firmament; and they that turn many to righteousness as the stars for ever and ever.* (Daniel 12:3)

Many today place too much emphasis on gaining earthly honor. They should desire to be a "star" in heaven rather than on earth. They seek fame, stardom, and the transitory praises of men. All too often, men seek after earthly walks of fame and celebrity status, which shall one day all perish in an instant. All one needs is to become a star in glory, eternally etched on the walls of God's hall of faith! (See Hebrews 11:1.) You can do this right now by simply asking Jesus to forgive you of your sins and by accepting Him as Lord and Savior. If you have not already, do

so today!

A Heavenly Body

In Jesus' day, there was a group of religious leaders called the Sadducees. This particular group of theologians did not even believe in the resurrection. This religious crowd was anti-miraculous, anti-supernatural, anti-God, and anti-heaven! And yet, they claimed to be sons of Abraham, Isaac, and Jacob. (See Matthew 22:23.) But Jesus said that God was the God of the living, not the dead!

> *Have you not read...I am the God of Abraham, and the God of Isaac, and the God of Jacob? God is not the God of the dead, but of the living. And when the multitude heard this, they were astonished at his doctrine.* (Matthew 22:32–33)

Again, we have seen that even Christ's own disciples, who had walked with Him for nearly three years, questioned the reality of a tangible resurrected body and the nature of heaven itself.

> *And as they thus spake, Jesus himself stood*

in the midst of them, and saith unto them, Peace be unto you. But they were terrified and affrighted, and supposed that they had seen a spirit. And he said unto them, Why are ye troubled? and why do thoughts arise in your hearts? (Luke 24:36–38)

The other disciples therefore said unto him, We have seen the Lord. But he said unto them, Except I shall see in his hands the print of the nails, and put my finger into the print of the nails, and thrust my hand into his side, I will not believe.... Then saith he to Thomas, Reach hither thy finger, and behold my hands; and reach hither thy hand, and thrust it into my side: and be not faithless, but believing. (John 20:25, 27)

Sadly, all too many Christians have a fear of death and erroneously assume that the Bible is unclear on the subjects of paradise and the resurrection. They wrongfully assume that the afterlife of a Christian is an "unknown." Many misinterpret 1 Corinthians 2:9, which says, *"Eye has not seen, nor ear heard, nor have entered into the heart of man the things which God has prepared for those who love Him"* (NKJV). Unfortunately, too many believers read that Scripture out of context and fail to read the very next verse. Oftentimes when we are reading the Bible, we can find the meaning of the text by simply reading verses that precede and follow the Scriptures at hand.

Thus, in this case, God is saying that although the heart of man in and of itself is not capable of understanding the glories of heaven, the Holy Spirit can reveal these truths to a believer whose spirit has been born again and who is sensitized to the spiritual significance of Bible doctrine. Note the following verses.

Eye hath not seen, nor ear heard, neither have entered into the heart of man, the things which God hath prepared for them that love him. But God hath revealed them unto us by his Spirit: for the Spirit searcheth all things, yea, the deep things of God. For what man knoweth the things of a man, save the spirit of man which is in him? even so the things of God knoweth no man, but the Spirit of God. Now we have received, not the spirit of the world, but the spirit which is of God; that we might know the things that are freely given to us of God.

(1 Corinthians 2:9–12)

God wants to open for you the very vault of heaven in these days so that you may see the treasures that await you! He desires for you to know the *"deep things of God."* He patiently waits for you to humble yourself and pray so that He can reveal the things that are freely given to you.

It is obviously true that there are many blessings and surprises in heaven that Christians on earth are currently unaware of. It is also true that a revelation of heaven cannot enter the heart of man without the influence of the Holy Spirit! That was a major point that the apostle Paul made to the brethren at Corinth. Heaven cannot be intellectually discerned but must be seen with the eye of faith. Paul knew that the Corinthians were carnally minded, yet he desperately wanted them to have a proper concept of the hereafter. The Word of God is spirit

and truth.

It is the spirit that quickeneth; the flesh profiteth nothing: the words that I speak unto you, they are spirit, and they are life.

(John 6:63)

For the word of God is quick, and powerful, and sharper than any twoedged sword, piercing even to the dividing asunder of soul and spirit, and of the joints and marrow, and is a discerner of the thoughts and intents of the heart.

(Hebrews 4:12)

The Word of God's noble and sacred doctrines are only unveiled through the power of the Holy Spirit. This includes the doctrine of heaven. In fact, compared to other major religions the Bible has far much more to say about heaven and paradise. Simply speaking, there are quite enough descriptions of this glorious place for us to consider here.

God has given us enough revelation to contemplate heaven in a way that is both edifying and informative. He knows our feeble frames. He knows how the fear of death has plagued human hearts and minds since the fall of Adam and Even, and He understands mankind's basic fear of death. It was because of sin that Adam and Eve fled from the presence of God and eternal life.

And they heard the voice of the LORD God walking in the garden in the cool of the day: and Adam and his wife hid themselves from the presence of the LORD God amongst the trees of the garden. And the LORD God called unto Adam, and said unto him, Where art thou?

(Genesis 3:8–9)

But they were terrified and affrighted, and supposed that they had seen a spirit. And he said unto them, Why are ye troubled? and why do thoughts arise in your hearts? Behold my hands and my feet, that it is I myself: handle me, and see; for a spirit hath not flesh and bones, as ye see me have. And when he had thus spoken, he showed them his hands and his feet. And while they yet believed not for joy, and wondered, he said unto them, Have ye here any meat? And they gave him a piece of a broiled fish, and of an honeycomb.

And he took it, and did eat before them.

(Luke 24:37–43)

Since the fall of Adam, mankind has feared everything from death to being alone in the dark. But Christ has now conquered not only the fear, but also death itself.

And deliver them who through fear of death were all their lifetime subject to bondage. (Hebrews 2:15)

Chapter Nine
God's Eternal Investment

God Protects His Investments

Did you know that certain Christian astrophysicists believe that God may have created the entire cosmos for the purpose of making life suitable for you and me on earth? Just think, the whole physical universe, with its billions of galaxies and solar systems, its intricate laws of biochemistry, energy, gravity, relativity, thermodynamics, etc., help to energize and organize the universe and ecosystem to make life suitable for every living creature on earth.

Yes, my friend, God has invested much in us! And embrace the truth that the uniqueness of your personality as a believer will be preserved forever. Listen, my friend, you are fearfully, wonderfully, and uniquely made!

You made all the delicate, inner parts of my body and knit me together in my mother's womb. Thank you for making me so wonderfully complex! Your workmanship is marvelous—and how well I know it. You watched me as I was being formed in utter seclusion, as I was woven together in the dark of the womb. You saw me before I was born. Every day of my life was recorded in your book. Every moment was laid out before a single day had passed. How precious are your thoughts about me, O God! They are innumerable!

(Psalm 139:13–17 NLT)

God will fully protect and preserve His investment in your body and soul. He will raise you again as an "eternally durable and sophisticated piece of workmanship!" And God gave the life of His own dear Son so that He could raise us up and freely give us *all things.*

He that spared not his own Son, but delivered him up for us all, how shall he not with him also freely give us all things? Who shall lay any thing to the charge of God's elect? It is God that justifieth.

(Romans 8:32–33)

God speaks of your personality and physical form as something He is quite proud of and very interested in preserving.

I am fearfully and wonderfully made: marvellous are thy works; and that my soul knoweth right well. (Psalm 139:14)

O Lord, thou hast searched me, and known me....Whither shall I go from thy spirit? or whither shall I flee from thy presence? If I ascend up into heaven, thou art there: if I make my bed in hell, behold, thou art there. (Psalm 139:1, 7–8)

Since your earthly body and personality are so precious to God, why would we think for a moment that He is not interested in preserving what He has already invested in us! Jesus has made free from the law of death and the sin principle everyone who believes in Him.

For the law of the Spirit of life in Christ Jesus hath made me free from the law of sin and death. (Romans 8:2)

Because of this, our earthly bodies *will be transformed* into heavenly bodies that will exist in a higher, and more perfected, state.

Behold, I show you a mystery; we shall not all sleep, but we shall all be changed, in a moment, in the twinkling of an eye, at the last trump: for the trumpet shall sound, and the dead shall be raised incorruptible, and we shall be changed.

(1 Corinthians 15:51–52)

The Bible says that flesh and blood cannot inherit the kingdom of God. (See John 3:1.) Sinful hearts must be cleansed through the blood of Calvary and born again by the Spirit of God. This is a work of the Holy Spirit and is not a physically orchestrated event by the will of man.

Jesus replied, "The truth is, no one can enter the Kingdom of God without being born of water and the Spirit. Humans can reproduce only human life, but the Holy Spirit gives new life from heaven. So don't be surprised at my statement that you must be born again. Just as you can hear the wind but can't tell where it comes from or where it is going, so you can't explain how people are born of the Spirit." "What do you mean?" Nicodemus asked. Jesus replied, "You are a respected Jewish teacher, and yet you don't understand these things? I assure you, I am telling you what we know and have seen, and yet you won't believe us. But if you don't even believe me when I tell you about things that happen here on earth, how can you possibly believe if I tell you what is going on in heaven?" (John 3:5–12 NLT)

But the Bible is also referring to the fact that our current earthly bodies, tainted from original sin, do not have the capacity to dwell in the glory-filled realms of heaven. *These earthly bodies are not capable of absorbing the love-energy and full light of the glory of God the Father.* Yet Jesus appeared after the resurrection to His disciples to show us that the resurrection body would be in a tangible and identifiable human form that captured one's unique features and appearance—a glorified likeness of our bodies that are now on earth.

My friend, the resurrection of a believer's body and his eternal identity is one of the greatest doctrines of the Christian faith. So don't be overly concerned when you hear certain misconceptions regarding the resurrected body.

But some man will say, How are the dead raised up? and with what body do they come? Thou fool, that which thou sowest is not quickened, except it die: and that which thou sowest, thou sowest not that body that shall be, but bare grain, it may chance of wheat, or of some other grain: but God giveth it a body as it hath pleased him, and to every seed his own body. (1 Corinthians 15:35–38)

So also is the resurrection of the dead. It is sown in corruption; it is raised in incorruption: it is sown in dishonour; it is raised in glory: it is sown in weakness; it is raised in power....In a moment, in the twinkling of an eye, at the last trump: for the trumpet shall sound, and the dead shall be raised incorruptible, and we shall be changed. (1 Corinthians 15: 42–43, 52)

The apostle Paul was a true man of God. He didn't mince words. He didn't care if he was noticed or if he was popular. It was not out of character for him to call some of the carnally minded believers of his day "foolish." These were those persons who were overly concerned, fearful, or confused regarding the resurrection body. Today he might be considered a "negative, doomsday, and legalistic preacher"—but that false accusation wouldn't bother him either. *You see, Paul had been to heaven!* (See 2 Corinthians 12:1.) Nothing on earth could shake him—especially public opinion! And a man with a genuine experience from God is never at the mercy of a man with an intellectual argument!

Fear Not

The doctrine of heaven and the doctrine of the bodily resurrection are both vital belief systems for the church, especially in this hour. As a believer, you do not need to fear anything—not even death itself. Death cannot touch a true believer. You may see its shadow but that is all. (See Psalm 23:4.) In Christ Jesus you will never lose for one moment your identity or your consciousness of self. You will only become more perfected and will have greater capacity to converse with

God Himself and the higher intelligences of heaven. All of this should constrain us to humility and cause us to rejoice!

Mysterious and Complex

Einstein once said that although God was mysterious and cryptic He was not malevolent.

> *Truly you are a God who hides himself, O God and Savior of Israel.* (Isaiah 45:15)

He has made no two people exactly alike. Even with the potential of human cloning there will never be another person exactly identical to another. Scientists tell us that even the blood vessels that make up the back of every person's eye and that supply blood to the retina are infinitely unique. Like an individual fingerprint or a specially designed snowflake, not one is alike. God's entire creation has been described by scientists as sheer "irreducible complexity."

This simply means that from the greatest galaxies down to the smallest living organisms one will find incredibly complex handiwork—the obvious fingerprints of a very intelligent Creator. Even the smallest of organisms is an extremely complex collection of molecules. God loves details. He is the ultimate artist! He is the ultimate inventor, scientist, mathematician, artist, physicist, doctor, and creator. All the best human endeavors on earth pale in comparison to His handiwork.

The human brain alone has more neurons than the entire universe has stars! The human body is the most magnificent example of "irreducible complexity" in the entire universe. He loves beauty and takes great pride and joy in His creative designs. We must never forget that Christianity is a religion of redemption where salvation is always linked to the body. We should always remember that God has made our individualized bodies for the purpose of eternal identity.

Like a Lost Child

For instance, just look at a little child who momentarily has been lost in a supermarket. There may be many sweet faces of mothers in that supermarket, but that young child will always beam with joy at the recognition of the face of *his own mother*. So it is with Jesus. There may be many different "faces" of false idols, false gods, and false shepherds. They come in all sizes and shapes. There are many voices out there in the world. But the child of God, the true sheep of the Lord, will only recognize the face and voice of the true Shepherd—even as they will be recognized by Him.

And when he putteth forth his own sheep, he goeth before them, and the sheep follow him: for they know his voice....I am the door: by me if any man enter in, he shall be saved, and shall go in and out, and find pasture....I am the good shepherd: the good shepherd giveth his life for the sheep....I am the good shepherd, and know my sheep, and am known of mine.
(John 10:4, 9, 11, 14)

The LORD is my shepherd; I shall not want. He maketh me to lie down in green pastures: he leadeth me beside the still waters....Surely goodness and mercy shall follow me all the days of my life: and I will dwell in the house of the LORD *for ever.* (Psalm 23:1–2, 6)

Even as a believer can recognize the sweet voice of the Good Shepherd while living on earth, so it is that when a believer departs, he will also instantly recognize heaven as his *home.*

God Is Down to Earth

God does not desire to "scare" anyone. The Bible says that God wants us to be of sound mind. That He wants us to have His peace.

For God hath not given us the spirit of fear; but of power, and of love, and of a sound mind. (2 Timothy 1:7)

He knows our feeble frames well! The father of fear, Satan, has dished out enough unhealthy fear, anxiety, and stress in these last days.

Men's hearts failing them for fear, and for looking after those things which are coming on the earth: for the powers of heaven

shall be shaken. (Luke 21:26)

I am so thankful that our Lord longs to take our anxiety and stress from us. Jesus longs to take our fear from us and to give us His peace.

Peace I leave with you, my peace I give unto you: not as the world giveth, give I unto you. Let not your heart be troubled, neither let it be afraid. (John 14:27)

Come unto me, all ye that labour and are heavy laden, and I will give you rest. Take my yoke upon you, and learn of me; for I am meek and lowly in heart: and ye shall find rest unto your souls. For my yoke is easy, and my burden is light.
(Matthew 11:28–30)

Jesus understands the fallen nature and weaknesses of mankind. He goes to great lengths to never cause us to fear. Even when He sends an angelic messenger, the angel usually begins His message by saying, "Fear not."

And, lo, the angel of the Lord came upon them, and the glory of the Lord shone round about them: and they were sore afraid. And the angel said unto them, Fear not: for, behold, I bring you good tidings of great joy, which shall be to all people. (Luke 2:9–10)

But the angel said unto him, Fear not, Zacharias: for thy prayer is heard; and thy wife Elisabeth shall bear thee a son, and thou shalt call his name John.

(Luke 1:13)

I've heard it said that God used the concept "fear not" in the Bible exactly 365 times—one for each day of the year!

The Post-Resurrection "Cookout"

The Word says that God has not given us a spirit of fear. God is not the author of fear. He longs to still the storms that, at times, arise in our hearts. This is why, after the resurrection, He purposely appeared to His disciples in His physical body on a beach along the Sea of Galilee. Here, on a peaceful seashore, the Prince of Peace would calm their stormy hearts once again. (See Mark 4:39.) It should be

no surprise for us that Jesus encouraged His disciples with a post-resurrection "cookout." Understanding their fragile hearts, He joyfully summoned them to eat some of the wood-fired, grilled fish and freshly cooked bread He had prepared for them.

Then Jesus saith unto them, Children, have ye any meat? They answered him, No....As soon then as they were come to land, they saw a fire of coals there, and fish laid thereon, and bread. Jesus saith unto them, Bring of the fish which ye have now caught. Simon Peter went up, and drew the net to land full of great fishes, an hundred and fifty and three: and for all there were so many, yet was not the net broken. Jesus saith unto them, Come and dine. And none of the disciples durst ask him, Who art thou? knowing that it was the Lord. (John 21:5, 9–12)

He especially understood doubting Thomas' heart and later appeared to him challenging Thomas to physically touch Him.

Then saith he to Thomas, Reach hither thy finger, and behold my hands; and reach hither thy hand, and thrust it into my side: and be not faithless, but believing. And Thomas answered and said unto him, My Lord and my God.

(John 20:27–28)

He wanted them to know that He was no ghost and that He was His own familiar self. Even after the resurrection, His body was intact and His identity was familiar to him. He longs to calm our fears and still our wants. Jesus is a "down-to-earth" God.

Still Enough to Hear His Voice

God wants to speak to each and every one of us of His great love. He wants to show us in our spirits the glories of heaven. The voice of Jesus is so kind and peaceful. His voice is sweet and still. How familiar are you with His voice? Can you recognize His voice from all the others? Are you "still" enough to hear Him? For if our hearts are yielded and still and tranquil enough, we can hear His still small voice—if we intercede, fast, and pray and more earnestly seek His face. If we imbibe of His Word daily and drink of the golden nectar of His sweet Holy Spirit, God is more than willing to speak to us and to preview for us the glories that are to come for those who are longing for His appearing.

But God hath revealed them unto us by his Spirit: for the Spirit searcheth all things, yea, the deep things of God.

(1 Corinthians 2:10)

There are *conditions* for us if we are to clearly hear His voice. And a worshipper must foremost know His voice. One condition is to be possessed with a sense of *longing*. We are to long for and look for His appearing.

Henceforth there is laid up for me a crown of righteousness, which the Lord, the righteous judge, shall give me at that day: and not to me only, but unto all them also that love his appearing. (2 Timothy 4:8)

Another is to *abide in Him*. For if we continually abide in His presence, we will bear much fruit and will walk in the miraculous.

Abide in me, and I in you. As the branch cannot bear fruit of itself, except it abide in the vine; no more can ye, except ye abide in me. I am the vine, ye are the branches: He that abideth in me, and I in him, the same bringeth forth much fruit: for without me ye can do nothing.
(John 15:4–5)

If we abide in Him, we shall also enjoy the "fruit" of pure worship! And if we are still enough to abide in Him, we will learn to perceive His still small voice with greater accuracy.

And he said, Go forth, and stand upon the mount before the LORD. And, behold, the LORD passed by, and a great and strong wind rent the mountains, and brake in pieces the rocks before the LORD; but the LORD was not in the wind: and after the wind an earthquake; but the LORD was not in the earthquake: and after the earthquake a fire; but the LORD was not in the fire: and after the fire a still small voice.
(1 Kings 19:11–12)

A lot of people look for powerful manifestations, but God is looking for hearts that are quiet and still before Him.

And that ye study to be quiet.
(1 Thessalonians 4:11)

The key to hearing His voice is to be quiet enough and still enough to listen.

For thus saith the Lord GOD, the Holy One of Israel; In returning and rest shall ye be saved; in quietness and in confidence shall

be your strength: and ye would not.
(Isaiah 30:15)

God considers a heart that is not "still" virtually unteachable. For anyone who cannot hear the gentle voice of Jesus cannot possibly be abiding in Him. And if they cannot abide in Him, how can they do His will?

But the wicked are like the troubled sea, when it cannot rest, whose waters cast up mire and dirt. There is no peace, saith my God, to the wicked. (Isaiah 57:20–21)

Dear saint, as you read this book and listen to this music, quietly pray for God to open up your spiritual eyes to see and ears to listen. He longs to speak to each of His people. He wants us to begin to recognize His sweet and lovely voice and to know that all the promises of God are yes and amen. This includes His promise of the joy and ecstasy of heaven.

For all the promises of God in him are yea, and in him Amen, unto the glory of God by us. (2 Corinthians 1:20)

In summary, we have seen that our resurrection body will be similar to Christ's own resurrection body. (See 1 Corinthians 15:20, 23; Colossians 1:18; Revelation 1:5; Romans 8:23; 1 Corinthians 6:13–20.) The "shell" of the old earthly/natural body will be reconstituted and replaced with a new heavenly substance—a new spiritual body of light! This resurrection body will have unimaginable capacities and giftings. Yes, my beloved friend, you are someone special. And God has invested much in your creation and does not so easily give up on His hard-earned investments!

Chapter Ten
The Heavenlies

And hath raised us up together, and made us sit together in heavenly places in Christ Jesus.   (Ephesians 2:6)

The Heavenly Places

Some may ask, "Where are these heavenly places? How do we know they're really there?" Because the Bible says that they exist. I used to wonder if heaven was located in a different spiritual dimension of reality, a dimension existing on a higher plane. Regardless of how the heavenly places exist through God's power, while we are on this earth we will need spiritual eyes to see into this realm.

It is obvious that unless there is a special visitation from God, such as a theophany or a christophany (this is where Christ physically appeared to a believer in the Old Testament—as with Abraham, Moses, Daniel), we will need to "see" Christ in heaven with the spiritual eyes of faith.

This walk of faith does not involve our physical eyesight, nor does it rely upon the other four senses.

Heaven Is Axiomatic!

The axiomatic truths of divine Scripture and revelation exist independently of our own existence. God's reality exists whether we believe in Him or not. Heaven exists whether or not you or I believe in it. Believe me, the truths of the Bible will always be a reality—even if we were no longer here to perceive them! The kingdom of God will go on with or without us. When the apostle Peter received a revelation that Jesus was the Son of God, he must have heard the word of the Lord in his spirit because Jesus said that "flesh and blood" had not revealed this to him. You see, faith resides above the five senses. Some of you call it a sixth sense, but I do not care to put it on the same level as the sensory perceptions of the human body. And faith only comes by hearing the Word of the Lord.

So then faith cometh by hearing, and

hearing by the word of God.

(Romans 10:17)

Human science depends on observation, generally through the five senses. But the five physical senses are no reliable guide to our faith. The Scriptures have taught us that only through the eyes of faith can we see into the heavenly realms, only the Word of God is a sure guide, and flesh and blood cannot inherit the kingdom of heaven.

I declare to you, brothers, that flesh and blood cannot inherit the kingdom of God, nor does the perishable inherit the imperishable. (1 Corinthians 15:50 NIV)

It is the spirit that quickeneth; the flesh profiteth nothing: the words that I speak unto you, they are spirit, and they are life. (John 6:63)

Saint Augustine once said, "I do not understand in order to believe, but I believe in order that I might understand."

It is true that the original disciples physically dwelt with Jesus while He was on earth and perceived Him empirically with their five senses.

That which was from the beginning, which we have heard, which we have seen with our eyes, which we have looked upon, and our hands have handled, of the Word of life; (for the life was manifested, and we have seen it, and bear witness, and show unto you that eternal life, which was with the Father, and was manifested unto us).

(1 John 1:1-2)

During the time Jesus was on the earth, believers experienced Christ with their five senses. But for the majority of believers, God requires us to exercise our eyes of faith. Jesus told Thomas that any person who believed in Him and had not physically seen Him was more blessed than those who saw Him physically in person.

Jesus saith unto him, Thomas, because thou hast seen me, thou hast believed: blessed are they that have not seen, and yet have believed. (John 20:29)

This is because a believer who solely

trusts in the resurrected Christ through the spiritual sense of faith bases that faith solely from hearing the Word.

Now faith is the substance of things hoped for, the evidence of things not seen.

(Hebrews 11:1)

But without faith it is impossible to please him: for he that cometh to God must believe that he is, and that he is a rewarder of them that diligently seek him.

(Hebrews 11:6)

Through faith there is a great recompense of reward. (See Hebrews 10:35.) It is fascinating to consider that the Bible teaches that faith is both a fruit and a gift of the Holy Spirit. Only faith allows believers to "see" the things of heaven. Let me repeat, it is common to hear Scriptures misquoted and taken out of context in regard to what God has said concerning the matter of a believer's ability to catch a glimpse of heaven.

But as it is written, Eye hath not seen, nor ear heard, neither have entered into the heart of man, the things which God hath prepared for them that love him. But God hath revealed them unto us by his Spirit: for the Spirit searcheth all things, yea, the deep things of God.

(1 Corinthians 2:9–10)

Again, let me reiterate to you, my friend, that most good Christians only quote the first Scripture of this text, and they fail to read and understand verse 10. But how are these things revealed to us? Paul said that it is through the Holy Spirit, who gives faith as both a fruit and a gift from God! It is by faith that we can see the *"substance of things hoped for."* The Bible says that through the power of the Holy Spirit, we can see the things that God has prepared for those who love Him!

That the God of our Lord Jesus Christ, the Father of glory, may give unto you the spirit of wisdom and revelation in the knowledge of him: the eyes of your understanding being enlightened; that ye may know what is the hope of his calling, and what the riches of the glory of his inheritance in the saints.

(Ephesians 1:17–18)

FAITH

The Holy Spirit has freely given all earnest and prayerful believers the potential for "revelatory eyesight." He has given us eyes of faith whereby we are able to see beyond this present world. He has given us all a spiritual sense where we are able to see into the spiritual realms, even the glory and power of God.

Pray for Vision

Pray in Jesus' name for heavenly vision. Many great saints will testify that they received powerful revelations from God that came to them after they *prayed* and *fasted*. Prayer and fasting creates an atmosphere of spiritual calmness and luminosity. In this sublime spiritual state, a believer will become receptive to hear the voice of God, to see visions and to have dreams. There is no amount of human will and creativity that will cause us to see. There exists no telescope or human technology that can peer into this realm. We need the help of the Holy Spirit and His gift of faith. We need to surrender to God in prayer.

For how else could the prophets of old see the plan of God hundreds of years in advance of when the actual events happened?

For the prophecy came not in old time by the will of man: but holy men of God spake as they were moved by the Holy Ghost. (2 Peter 1:21)

In other words, a believer just can't "work up" a vision or a dream. Such a vision of heaven cannot be generated with the human mind or intellect. For the soul has already been stained through original sin and its fallen nature does not desire to contemplate either the exalted position of Christ or the substances of heaven. No, my friend, in order to see into that realm and in order to know the future through God's eyes, we must depend on the Holy Spirit to give us sight.

Which things also we speak, not in the words which man's wisdom teacheth, but which the Holy Ghost teacheth; comparing spiritual things with spiritual. But the natural man receiveth not the things of the

Spirit of God: for they are foolishness unto him: neither can he know them, because they are spiritually discerned.

(1 Corinthians 2:13–14)

For didn't even the apostle write this testimony to the Hebrews?

But without faith it is impossible to please him: for he that cometh to God must believe that he is, and that he is a rewarder of them that diligently seek him. By faith Noah, being warned of God of things not seen as yet, moved with fear, prepared an ark to the saving of his house....By faith Abraham...was called to go out into a place....For he looked for a city which hath foundations, whose builder and maker is God....These all died in faith, not having received the promises, but having seen them afar off, and were persuaded of them, and embraced them, and confessed that they were strangers and pilgrims on the earth. For they that say such things declare plainly that they seek a country.... But now they desire a better country, that is, an heavenly: wherefore God is not ashamed to be called their God: for he hath prepared for them a city.

(Hebrews 11:6–8, 10, 13–14, 16)

Protective, Spiritual "Eyeglasses"

How else could Noah proactively take measures to preserve himself and his family from the coming storm? In other words, Noah could clearly "see" the future plan of God for his life and family through the eyes of faith. Do you see God's destiny and plan for your life? Do you see the coming storm and are you preparing for it? Can you see the Holy City and the New Jerusalem being prepared and now descending from the heavens toward earth? Abraham could see the Holy City and the New Jerusalem over four thousand years ago!

I ask you, my dear friend, what do you see? Jesus said we must be pure in heart in order that we might see Him. Can you see Jesus high and lifted up with His train filling the temple? The pure prophet Isaiah could.

In the year that king Uzziah died I saw

also the Lord sitting upon a throne, high and lifted up, and his train filled the temple. Above it stood the seraphims: each one had six wings; with twain he covered his face, and with twain he covered his feet, and with twain he did fly. And one cried unto another, and said, Holy, holy, holy, is the LORD *of hosts: the whole earth is full of his glory.* (Isaiah 6:1–3)

Chapter Eleven
Seeing Jesus

No Respecter of Persons

Anyone who loves God and who is prayerful, anyone who is humble and who is pure in heart, can "see" Christ. For God is no respecter of persons.

Then Peter opened his mouth, and said, Of a truth I perceive that God is no respecter of persons. (Acts 10:34)

And if ye call on the Father, who without respect of persons judgeth according to every man's work, pass the time of your sojourning here in fear. (1 Peter 1:17)

We here at Golden Altar Records do not claim to have arrived, nor do we claim any privileged position, new revelation, or inspiration. It is only by God's grace and through His Holy Spirit that He allows any believer to see into the glory realms of Christ. To have a vision, a visitation, or a dream from God does not necessarily make anyone "better" as a Christian.

It should not make anyone think they are more spiritual just because other believers haven't had such experiences. As a matter of fact, having an encounter with the Lord will make you more accountable to God and will put a healthy fear of the Lord in you!

For what is man that God is even mindful of him? For all that pertains to godliness and salvation is found in the holy, inerrant, and infallible sixty-six books of the Bible—our only reliable source for spiritual doctrine, truth, and salvation.

But he answered and said, It is written, Man shall not live by bread alone, but by every word that proceedeth out of the mouth of God. (Matthew 4:4)

Yet God still invites sincere believers to come up hither and "see."

After this I looked, and, behold, a door was opened in heaven: and the first voice which I heard was as it were of a trumpet talking with me; which said, Come up hither, and I will show thee things which must be hereafter. (Revelation 4:1)

Jesus answered and said unto him, Because I said unto thee, I saw thee under the fig tree, believest thou? thou shalt see greater things than these. And he saith unto him, Verily, verily, I say unto you, Hereafter ye shall see heaven open, and the angels of God ascending and descending upon the Son of man.

(John 1:50–51)

For those who make a covenant with their eyes not to look upon evil; for those who love purity and holiness; to the pure in heart, God promises divine eyesight that can see Jesus in all of His glory.

Blessed are the pure in heart: for they shall see God. (Matthew 5:8)

If visions and dreams are given to us by the Lord, they should always cause us to become more humble and kind. In other words, the vision or experience should point to Jesus and Jesus alone—lest we become prideful and puffed up because of the revelations given to us.

It is not expedient for me doubtless to glory. I will come to visions and revelations of the Lord. I knew a man in Christ above fourteen years ago, (whether in the body, I cannot tell; or whether out of the body, I cannot tell: God knoweth;) such an one caught up to the third heaven. And I knew such a man, (whether in the body, or out of the body, I cannot tell: God knoweth;) how that he was caught up into paradise, and heard unspeakable words, which it is not lawful for a man to utter. Of such an one will I glory: yet of myself I will not glory, but in mine infirmities. For though I would desire to glory, I shall not be a fool; for I will say the truth: but now I forbear, lest any man should think of me above that which he seeth me to be, or that he heareth of me.

(2 Corinthians 12:1–6)

Like Paul, all of us need humility, which will give us the capacity to be used of God in this hour. Otherwise, do not ask God for a vision of heaven—it will only get you a "thorn in the flesh" if you become prideful about the whole thing. At worst, you yourself might become a "thorn" to others because of your headiness.

In the following Scripture, we see that Paul thoroughly learned his lesson about supernatural revelations, visions, and visitations with the Lord.

> *And lest I should be exalted above measure through the abundance of the revelations, there was given to me a thorn in the flesh, the messenger of Satan to buffet me, lest I should be exalted above measure.*
>   (2 Corinthians 12:7)

Chapter Twelve

Real Power on Earth

Why is a vision of heaven important for believers in this hour? I believe that a vision of heaven can encourage us all for the following reasons:

- First, you will be inspired to win souls, heal the sick, and raise the dead. (See Mark 16:16–20.) To be heavenly minded is to desire that no one misses out on eternal life. You need to have a heavenly perspective that will burden you to win souls and will cause you to get about the business of the Great Commission. (See Matthew 28:18–20.) Rather than being motivated to preach the gospel only from the perspective of trying to keep souls out of hell, your approach will be augmented by a more pure and more positive motivation. The blessed goal is that we as believers do not want *anyone* to miss out on the joys and glories of paradise! (See Luke 16:23; 23:43.)

- Second, getting a vision of heaven will help you become a prophetic believer. Like Ezekiel, you will be able to prophesy to the "dead bones" of the alcoholic, the drug addict, the sex addict, etc., so that those in bondage can be freed from being servants of corruption and thus be cleansed and empowered and made alive by God's grace. (See Ezekiel 36:1.) You need to believe that through faith you can connect with the unlimited heavenly realm above. (See Romans 4:17; Hebrews 11:1.) For there is no lack in heaven. For in heaven there are new limbs and organs for sick bodies. (See Mark 11:23–24.) There is plenty of provision and wealth for those who are in need. (See Philippians 4:19.) There is forgiveness and deliverance from sin. But only those with prophetic vision will be able to see into this exalted, unlimited realm. By having spiritual vision, you will also become more sensitive to the needs of others and will flow in the power of God so that they can be set free from their bondage and be empowered and animated by God's grace and His Holy Spirit to lead a life worth living in Christ.

- Third, you need a vision of heaven so that you can see your own need to die to self and come to the cross. (See Romans 6:1-8.) Then, God's presence will fill your home as His glory comes down, and His heavenly presence will empower you to live in this world with great love and power. (See Acts 2:1-38.) Since heaven is such a wealthy, powerful, and abundant place, a lot of earthly good can be done when we connect with our home above. (See Matthew 6:9; Luke 11:2.) To be heavenly minded is to see the great need and poverty of fallen mankind. (See Isaiah 6:8.) Therefore, we need a divine contrast so that we will want to do something great for God that will change the earth for the glory of Christ. We're not talking about adhering to some form of "passive pietism" here.

- Fourth, to see into heaven is to catch a glimpse of the precious blood of Christ sprinkled on the mercy seat in the eternal temple of God. (See Hebrews 9:12-18.) It is also to see that heaven is a better country where there is real authority over evil. (See Hebrews 11:1-18.) To see the power of Christ's blood eternal in the heavens is to know your authority on earth where, in the name of Jesus, you can speak to mountains and they will be moved. (See Mark 11:23-24.)

- Fifth, to have a vision of heaven is to catch a vision that one day soon we all will stand before God's great and lofty throne and before the twenty-four elders. (See Revelation 7:9-12.) There each and every one of us will give an account of every thought, imagination, word, and deed. All that we are will be weighed in the balance in the pure light of His eternal justice. (See Matthew 12:36; Luke 16:2; Romans 14:12; Hebrews 13:17.)

■ Sixth, to be heavenly minded is to see the omnipotence and majesty of the God of Glory, who spoke all the worlds into being. (See Genesis 1:1-2; Hebrews 11:3.) Such a vision will naturally instill in us a sense of childlike wonder and will cause us to walk in great humility and gratefulness before the Lord. In other words, to see heaven will instill in each of us a divine feeling of "awe" and amazement.

For the reasons above, I believe Paul could boldly say, "*Set your affection on things above, not on things on the earth*" (Colossians 3:2)!

Chapter Thirteen
The Heavenly Bride

The Sacred Romance

There's going to be a wedding in heaven! The Bridegroom is coming! May all of us begin to get oil in our lamps. May all of us ready our hearts in passionate love and adoration of Him. May the Holy Spirit fill us as He beckons us to enter the holiest place in worship, for this is the only sure place of spiritual safety. (See Matthew 25:1.) For His presence is a strong tower and a place of refuge in these trying times when men's hearts will wax cold and will fail them for fear of things that are about to come on the earth. Yet as the Holy Spirit gently beckons us, His bride, to draw close to Him, it is in this secret place of intimacy that we will find true *spiritual immunity*.

It is in the secret place of intimate worship that we will find renewed strength, prosperity, provision, rest, peace, endurance, courage, healing, salvation, and deliverance. It is in this private place of prayer and worship that we will become more than conquerors through Him who loves us. It is also from this secret place of power that God will empower His army with a heavenly commission to win all the nations to Christ! God is longing to fulfill His destiny for you and help you catch a glimpse of what His victorious church is about to see and behold.

Ardent Love

We are to be a bride ardently in love with Him, a bride holy and pure unto Him. God's desire is to restore us in holy love to be like His Second Adam. You see, the Father's desire is to enlarge His celestial family by restoring us as the glorious gleaming sons and daughters of the new Eden—robed in His pure light. We are to continually dwell with Him in the garden of God as in the cool of the day.

The Father's greatest desire is to restore us to moral perfection and purity. He does this as we yield to His grace. His grace conforms us to His own image if we but allow it to do so. Jesus longs to recreate His own image in each of us and to restore us to the virginal purity of paradise that was lost through Adam's fall and through original sin. And by His enabling grace, He can set us free from the temptation of sin or any desire of the knowledge of it or interest in it! There is such a place in Christ.

Jesus prayed that we would not be led into temptation and that we would be delivered from evil. It is time for the bride to become intoxicated with His love, to put on pure eyes, pure ears, pure thoughts, and pure deeds—in short, to put on Christlikeness.

The supreme goal of the Father is to conform many sons and daughters into the image of His own dear Son. He must clothe our moral nakedness and fallen carnal nature with the righteousness and pure virginal light of Christ. By His grace we may simply yield to Him, asking Him for help so that we can attain without much difficulty at all! The Father longs to see His Son reflected back to Him through the mirror of His church. But the false religious fire of vain ambition has darkened the mirror. All of us now should humble ourselves, as Christ did, and yield ourselves to become partakers of His divine nature.

Whereby are given unto us exceeding great and precious promises: that by these ye might be partakers of the divine nature, having escaped the corruption that is in the world through lust. (2 Peter 1:4)

It matters not what gross sin or crime you may have committed up until now. Today you can repent. Today is the day of salvation, grace, and forgiveness.

For he saith, I have heard thee in a time accepted, and in the day of salvation have I succoured thee: behold, now is the accepted time; behold, now is the day of salvation. (2 Corinthians 6:2)

Jesus' blood can cleanse you from any sin. It is true that God will not "wink" at your sin. It's not okay to sin, and there is great risk of eternal loss to a soul who loves sin. But God's grace is sufficient!

Simply throw yourself at His feet and you will find mercy, help, and grace in time of need.

> *Let us therefore come boldly unto the throne of grace, that we may obtain mercy, and find grace to help in time of need.*
> (Hebrews 4:16)

The Father is preparing many daughters and sons for a holy and priestly wedding ceremony. Yet many souls await the message of the good news of salvation and needlessly dwell in the valley of shadows. Jesus, our Emmanuel, the Daystar from on high, has visited us with His great light, as He is searching diligently for His faithful bride.

The Priestly Bride

In Anna Rountree's book, *The Priestly Bride*, Jesus tells the church that she is to become His eyes, His hands, His voice, His feet, and His heart on this earth. For what does a priest do but represent the people to God? In the Old Testament, the priest was commanded to "stand in" for the people before God. As New Testament believers, we are now called priests of God.

> *And hast made us unto our God kings and priests: and we shall reign on the earth.* (Revelation 5:10)
>
> *But ye are a chosen generation, a royal priesthood.* (1 Peter 2:9)

The priestly bride is not just a bride who is sitting around waiting for her Bridegroom, but she is one who is busily preparing for Him.

Peter said that we, as priests unto God, are to show forth His praises so those who dwell in darkness can also see His great light. (See verse 9.) In other words, the heavenly bride is also a warrior bride, a priestly bride—a bride who represents Jesus to those who are without Christ. The priestly bride is a bride who will stand in the gap in prayer and intercession and who will actively and aggressively war against the enemy by engaging in spiritual warfare.

The priestly bride is an overcoming

bride—that is, she destroys the works of the enemy. The Word says that the gates of hell will not prevail against this end-times bride, who is the church triumphant. Surrendering our lives totally to Christ and allowing Jesus to manifest His very nature through us in order to touch others with the gospel—this is truly being a priestly bride.

A Heavenly Wedding

Jesus is proposing to each and every one of us in this hour. As we accept, He gives us His righteousness. The apostle Paul promised the church that Christ will prepare for Himself a bride without spot or wrinkle. The Greek word for spotless is *spilos*, which means "one having no sin and without moral blemish." And when Jesus taught us in the gospels to be perfect as His heavenly Father is perfect, He was not just referring to our spiritual maturity but to the ability of His grace to produce moral perfection in His yielded children. For grace is God's enabling power working within us to be what He's called us to be and to do what He's called us to do.

> *For it is God which worketh in you both to will and to do of his good pleasure.*
> (Philippians 2:13)

> *For by grace are ye saved through faith; and that not of yourselves: it is the gift of God.* (Ephesians 2:8)

The true bride of Christ will be full of God's grace. We will no longer have any desire for evil and our lives will be pure.

Heavenly Perfection

Today, there are too many Christians who keep confessing that they cannot possibly keep from sinning. They say something like, "Sure, I sin. I'm just a sinner saved by grace." This argument, with its low standard and benchmark, is both unbiblical and unacceptable.

Just because most professed Christians do not live a morally perfect life does not prove that such a holy life is unattainable, for all is possible with God through His grace.

Many try to get around Jesus' message of perfection by saying the word *perfect* simply means "to be mature." When you ask them what they mean by mature, they don't really seem to know. But the word perfect in Scripture means for one to live without moral blemish, sin, or fault. God has given us the divine means and ability not to willfully sin. The lure of sin and evil will never be greater than the blood of Jesus, the name of Jesus, and the grace of God! God forbid if they were!

This is not to say that all Christians are perfect and that believers never sin. But the standard is still what it is. If a person repents, it is obvious that a moral failure or mistake will not keep him out of heaven. God is so merciful and kind. But there are sins that, if continued in, will lead to death. The Bible says there is a sin unto death. But a true saint will live life with joy and exuberance, not willing to offend God in any way.

I guess what some mean when they say someone is immature is that they continually sin but still are born again. At judg-ment, you know they hope that this is the case. The question I have is, Why would anyone who truly loves God hold this position? Of course every sinner loves to justify himself by using the grace of God in a precarious way. But the spiritually mature, the truly "perfect," will at some point not continue to willfully, deliberately, and habitually sin against God.

Perfection. Yes, there is such a blessed spiritual state; but we are not talking about some fastidious, legalistic concept of perfectionism by works. What we are talking about is the perfect disposition of the heart that has been Spirit-formed to the point where the soul, by the grace of God, no longer desires to fulfill the sinful lusts of the flesh.

No Willful Offense in God

When speaking about Christian perfection, I think Brother Lawrence has given us a balanced and proper perspective on the subject and has done so without *dodging* the issue of living morally pure before God:

We should be considerate of God in everything we do and say. Our goal should be to become perfect in our adoration of Him throughout this earthly life in preparation for all eternity. We must make a firm resolution to overcome, with God's grace, all the difficulties encountered in a spiritual life. From the very beginning of our Christian walk, we should remember who we are and that we are unworthy of the name of Christian except for what Christ has done for us...we must believe with certainty that it is both pleasing to God and good for us to sacrifice ourselves for Him. Without this complete submission of our hearts and minds to His will, He cannot work in us to make us perfect. The more we aspire to be perfect, the more dependent we are on the grace of God. We begin to need His help with every little thing and at every moment, because without it we can do nothing. The world, the flesh and the devil wage a fierce and continuous war on our souls. If we weren't capable of humbly depending on God for assistance, our souls would be dragged down. Although this total dependence may sometimes go against our human nature, God takes great pleasure in it. This should bring us rest. —Brother Lawrence

In other words, Brother Lawrence was saying that there is a "divine synergy" between the spirit of holiness and the Spirit of grace. One is dependent on the other for its efficacy.

Therefore, for a professed believer to deliberately and willfully and habitually sin while claiming Christ as Savior is a contradiction. For if the grace of God was truly at work in the heart, the old Adamic nature would not get the upper hand so easily. There is this dynamic tension between God's grace and Christian perfection. For us to walk "perfect" before the Lord, we must depend on His grace, but depending on His grace does not absolve us from our responsibility to surrender and submit continually to His grace so as not to offend Him or grieve His Holy Spirit by our lifestyle.

God's grace *is amazing*—for grace will cause a true believer not to offend or continually or willfully sin against God in any area of his life. This is Christian maturity. It seems today that the doctrine of holiness is under constant attack. People act like you must either choose between the "grace gospel" or the "holiness gospel." Some have even tried to make the blessed doctrine of holiness something that is boring, negative, or psychologically debilitating. They act like living a life of holiness will lead to a self-flagellating, beaten-down life that will lead to low self-esteem.

We must remember that Christian maturity is not based upon one's education or how many years someone has believed in Christ. Rather, Christian maturity is defined as how obedient one is to the voice of the Father; it is defined in regard to how much a person hates sin and loves righteousness and how obedient and yielded his will is to the Father's will. For without obedience, deep spiritual knowledge and an assortment of "deep teachings" will lead nowhere.

Holiness has always been the true standard for Christ's bride, and His grace is more than sufficient if we will but yield to it. For with God all things are possible—if we believe. The apostle Paul wrote to the church at Rome, "That which is not of faith is sin." (See Romans 14:23.) Jesus taught us to be perfect even as our heavenly Father is perfect. Oh, please, let us not charge God with unrighteousness and unfairness. You may say, "Yes, but nobody can live holy in this day and age." This is rubbish, and God is not unrighteous!

Holiness Does Not Injure

Finney asked the question, "Does holiness injure the soul?" Some modern evangelical psycho-babblists would answer him, "Yes." No wonder the church and culture is so backslidden. No wonder our own country is losing the cultural war against carnally minded liberals who have no moral core.

People who say that Christians cannot live a perfect and godly life are insulting our heavenly Father. For example, if an earthly father would give us standards, rules, or laws that we could *never* possibly obey and yet would punish us for not obeying them, we would consider this type of parent to be abusive and cruel. Yet our heavenly Father has given us the means of grace and has put within us that Divine Enabler who can live a holy life through us if we but surrender to His will. Don't believe the false prophets and teachers who are ever present on Christian radio and television and who preach false grace.

Yield to Him Today

The key to becoming a pure and chaste bride is to yield yourself to Him today. Don't delay this decision any longer. You may ask, How do I live above sin? How can I be free? Watchman Nee, in his book entitled *The Normal Christian Life,* taught that the key to living a holy life is simply what the apostle had learned—that *one must daily reckon himself or herself dead to the old nature and alive unto Christ!* (See Romans 6:11.)

You see, faith will take Christ at His word. In the book of Romans, one can clearly see Paul's personal transformation from a struggling Christian in chapter seven to a victorious, overcoming, sanctified believer in chapter eight. The key that unlocked his victory was the understanding that his righteousness was based on his total dependence on the Holy Spirit, who fully released in his life the force of the law of life and liberty in Christ Jesus.

For the law of the Spirit of life in Christ Jesus hath made me free from the law of sin and death. (Romans 8:2)

It is interesting to note that in chapter seven he made no mention of the Holy Spirit; rather, this chapter is peppered with the words *I, me,* and *my.* He was still trying to pull himself up by his bootstraps in a self-righteous, "do-good" mentality. This indicates to me that Paul's Jewish background of "works religion" had not been eradicated from his soul. He was still under the influence of a spirit of legalism and self-effort. He was trying to be holy through the power of his own will. But in chapter eight he replaced the words *I, me, my* with the word *Spirit.* He talked about receiving a salvation where his spirit bore witness with God's Spirit that he was a child of God.

No more doubts—Paul had learned to yield to the Spirit's grace. And after attaining this glorious state, the apostle never taught that living a holy life of perfect obedience to God is unattainable. He did say that he wished he could do more for God in his ministry and was only unfulfilled in that sense. In other words, Paul was referring to his goals in ministry rather than his moral or personal conduct. The key, he said, is that we must die to self and allow the Spirit to live and operate through us.

> *I am crucified with Christ: nevertheless I live; yet not I, but Christ liveth in me: and the life which I now live in the flesh I live by the faith of the Son of God, who loved me, and gave himself for me.*
>
> (Galatians 2:20)

A Heavenly Life on Earth

Do you want to live a heavenly life on earth? Paul said that if you want to live this way, it must be accomplished through the power of the Holy Spirit. But you must totally yield. The fruits of righteousness are not ours in the first place—they are the fruit of the Holy Spirit.

> *But the fruit of the Spirit is love, joy, peace, longsuffering, gentleness, goodness, faith, meekness, temperance: against such there is no law. And they that are Christ's have crucified the flesh with the affections and lusts. If we live in the Spirit, let us also walk in the Spirit.*
>
> (Galatians 5:22-25)

What we must do is surrender—to allow Him to live a holy life in us. Purity and holiness and a consecrated lifestyle through the power of the Holy Spirit have everything to do with becoming a true worshipper and a true, consecrated, priestly bride! Let us therefore, as His priestly bride, stop making excuses to ourselves and to others in justifying any sins of omission or commission in our lives. Let us stop accepting such a low benchmark for Christian living.

God desires pure worshippers who will not just sing a reverent song but who will live a Christlike life. And God forbid that anyone who professes Christ yet lives in habitual sin, would think for a moment that he will be welcome at Christ's wedding feast.

> And I say unto you, that many shall come from the east and west, and shall sit down with Abraham, and Isaac, and Jacob, in the kingdom of heaven. But the children of the kingdom shall be cast out into outer darkness: there shall be weeping and gnashing of teeth.   (Matthew 8:11–12)

> And while they went to buy, the bridegroom came; and they that were ready went in with him to the marriage: and the door was shut. Afterward came also the other virgins, saying, Lord, Lord, open to us. But he answered and said, Verily I say unto you, I know you not. Watch therefore, for ye know neither the day nor the hour wherein the Son of man cometh.
> (Matthew 25:10–13)

From the beginning Christ has never been interested in sin, nor will He allow any habitual sinner to defile the peace and joy of heaven. Therefore, as His priestly bride, yield to Him now and present yourself to Him as a living and holy sacrifice acceptable to God.

> I beseech you therefore, brethren, by the mercies of God, that ye present your bodies a living sacrifice, holy, acceptable unto God, which is your reasonable service. And be not conformed to this world: but be ye transformed by the renewing of your mind, that ye may prove what is that good, and acceptable, and perfect, will of God.   (Romans 12:1–2)

Faith Works by Love

The true priestly bride will delay no longer in yielding to the Holy Spirit. The priestly bride will learn to walk seeing the world as Jesus sees it. He will walk in Jesus' loving-kindness and grace. The Bible says faith works by love. (See Galatians 5:6.) Thus, to have more faith, we need to fall more in love with Jesus! The apostle John, who was the most beloved disciple, was closest to our Lord's heart; therefore, he was one of the chosen three to behold His glory on the Mount of Transfiguration.

Have you learned to love Jesus above all else yet? Oh, pure bride of Christ, do you worship Him and lay your head upon His shoulder? Do you say, as did the apostle John, "There is no one else that I desire but You"? Bride of Christ, do you love Jesus for who He is? Or do you love Him for what He can do for you? To purely love God is the greatest good in the entire universe. Let's yield to His Holy Spirit of love and allow His grace to work within us. (See Philippians 4:13.) Let us now, as His pure bride, become true worshippers. (See John 17:22–23.)

Chapter Fourteen
Heavenly Worship

The Fragrance of Heaven

Heavenly worship will stir up the heavenly, ambrosial fragrances of Jesus! It will stir the celestial air so that we might smell the perfume of our Rose of Sharon—our beloved Jesus. As we seek Him with heavenly worship, may we also smell the fragrance of His divine presence, even the divine presence of the King, the Lily of the Valley, and the Fairest of Ten Thousand.

Palatial Gardens

Our ardent desire is to ascend upward into the brilliance of His splendor so that we might take a stroll through His heavenly botanical gardens in paradise. One glimpse will change your life forever. Heavenly worship can take us there. For His temple is full of illustrious, palatial gardens. Oh, to sit with Him upon His white, marbled loveseat and listen to cascading waters gently flowing down His three-tiered water fountain! Oh, to visit His glorious heavenly temple—the divine archetype of heaven! May we progress in our worship to ascend even to the temple of God. And as we pass the altar of sacrifice, and the table of showbread, and the lamp stand, let us reverently and fearfully draw near to the holy ark of God's glory. Heavenly worship can take us there.

You might be asking yourselves why a book about paradise is followed by a discussion on worship and features worship music. I have done this because it is my sincere belief that no true understanding of heaven can be realized until believers begin to practice God's heavenly presence on earth through pure, heavenly worship. Worship is the highest form of prayer and intercession. Worship is holy, unbroken communion with the Father. Heavenly worship will take us closer to God's throne in paradise—it will take us closer than anything else we can do on this earth. Of course, there are some conditions or "keys" that God has given us before we can approach Him. Understanding from the Scriptures what heaven is like will help us understand how to approach the living God the way the Word has prescribed.

In the Lord's Prayer, Jesus prayed that God's will would be done on earth as it is in heaven. Therefore, while we live on earth here and now, it is important for us to understand this heaven wherein God's will originates. We need to understand its operation and what the Scriptures say about this glorious place. God has given each of us a foretaste of heaven through the gift of the Holy Spirit, and only He can teach us what we need to know. Worship on earth should reflect the pattern of things in heaven.

Garden in Paradise, a Musical Journey

I love to sing of my risen Savior and tell of the glorious heaven where He dwells! I also love to sing about paradise and the love of God that will be there. The glory of the risen Christ and the beauty of God's heaven can be explored through worship, narrative, music, prophetic art, and Scripture. It is our earnest prayer that by getting a glimpse of the glory of the risen Christ and the beautiful heaven where He dwells, you will be changed forever!

The entire project contains music that will lift your soul up to God. Are you grieving? The message will help edify your faith and will encourage you. Are you happy? The joyous sounds of the music and message will also minister to you and increase your desire for a genuine visitation from God.

Heavenscapes

At Golden Altar Records, we realize that it is virtually impossible for any person to truly describe the unspeakable glories and ecstasies of heaven. But through the grace of God, we have humbly endeavored to give the body of Christ a tiny "musical glimpse" into eternal realms of glory. More than ever, it is time for the precious bride of Christ to learn a little more of the wonders of heaven where she will soon dwell. Now is the time for all true believers to know their Bridegroom in a greater way. It is now time to rise up alongside His fiery seraphim and to love, obey, and worship Him all the more passionately.

The purpose of our ministry's message is to challenge and encourage believers everywhere to seek and obey the Lord Jesus Christ—not to seek after angelic visitations, visions, dreams, and encounters with the Lord. When one wholeheartedly seeks the Lord, oftentimes God can reveal Himself or manifest Himself to that person in many ways of His own choosing. Most often God reveals Himself through the written Word and through the inner peace and witness of the Holy Spirit within us. However, there are occasions when God can supernaturally visit us as well. Again, if one who loves God and who ardently prays is granted by God's grace to have such an encounter with the Lord, it in no way makes him a "better Christian," nor does it entitle him to any special favor from God.

The Music

After all, instilling in God's people a sense of longing is what we are all about. Our mission is to encourage the listener to go to a new level of passion in worship—to acquire a fresh taste for more of His presence. At Golden Altar Records, we seek to rekindle a passion in God's people to experience more of His unconditional, agape love. *Again, it is a call for the bride of Christ to enter into a sacred romance with the Bridegroom.*

If we will but totally surrender to the Holy Spirit and allow Him to worship through us; if we will allow Him to put within us that deep sense of longing to pursue Him, to please Him, then He will empower us through the flames of His fiery presence to worship the Father with a pure spirit of truth. This will certainly bring us to the place where we will be able to sing with the fiery seraphim, "Holy, Holy, Holy," and at every new and ever-changing revelation of Him to cry, "Holy, Holy, Holy," again and again!

But the hour cometh, and now is, when the true worshippers shall worship the Father in spirit and in truth: for the Father seeketh such to worship him. God is a Spirit: and they that worship him must worship him in spirit and in truth.

(John 4:23-24)

Embark on a Celestial Journey

The time is short. In the twinkling of an eye our glorious Bridegroom is about to translate His entire church into the glory realm. I pray that this music gives you and your loved ones a tiny, little foretaste of what is to come.

It is my prayer that through the power of the Holy Spirit, we can embark on a musical journey into a new and refreshing place in God. For God is calling us all to a deeper consecration in this hour and is making ready a bride without spot or wrinkle for Himself!

That he might present it to himself a glorious church, not having spot, or wrinkle, or any such thing; but that it should be holy

and without blemish. (Ephesians 5:27)

All He requires of us is that we approach Him with a humble, obedient, childlike heart. Then, after we seek Him for a season, we will be able to quietly listen to His still small voice and we will love to reply to Him as well. It is vitally important, therefore, that we all learn to develop an intimate relationship with Him where we can learn to recognize His sweet voice. We must learn to love His presence and abide there. All of us should desire to become more familiar with His voice simply because we love Him so much! And as we listen to His gentle reply, we will worship Him all the more fervently.

It is our earnest desire to experience His lovely presence and to love Him more and more each moment. We should ardently worship our Bridegroom and love to dwell in His presence more than anything on this earth. We should earnestly seek His presence and love Him more and more each moment. We should worship our Bridegroom and love His divine presence more than all things combined. The Lord's perfections are truly beyond comprehension. He is wholly desirable, and to worship Him and serve Him is the highest honor and privilege for any believer. He is so perfect, desirable, and comely. Therefore, He deserves to be our entire passionate pursuit and desire!

The Ascent of Heavenly Worship

In our worship, we should all endeavor to see and love our glorified Jesus with greater focus. We need to see our Christ in His now beautified and glorified form. We need to ascend on high in order to comprehend His transcendent majesty. But how do we ascend? How do we ascend even while pilgrims on this earth? There are conditions. The way of ascent is through consecrated hearts, which continually offer up pure worship. If we truly want a vision of heaven and our Lord Jesus glorified, we should practice a purer form of holy worship—heavenly worship.

Sounds like Heaven!

You may ask, what is heavenly worship? First and foremost, *it is worship that originates from heaven itself.* Heavenly worship is not "earthly" but is pure and comes down from the Father of lights. Like the heavenly wisdom that the apostle James speaks of, heavenly worship is never sensual, confusing, or vain. (See James 3:15–18.) It will not host a loud and raucous, seductive spirit. It is not performance-oriented, neither is it entertainment-oriented.

Heavenly worship is the highest form of intercession. It is an expression of true spiritual love for God in its most passionate, celebrated, and noble form. It is not to be trifled with. Heavenly worship is peaceable and heavenly worship is pure. Heavenly worship is glorious and heavenly worship carries with it the weighty presence of the Lord.

Only the pure of heart can worship God. Much of what is called "worship" today is actually not heavenly at all! Sadly, much of what is called "worship" and too much of what is both seen and heard today is earthly and sensual. There is too much of men's presence in it and not enough of God's! In some extreme cases, what some call "worship" has tragically become dark and evil in its expression. You see, earthy "worship" is a cheap, commercial imitation of the true form.

True worship is not just an expression of human emotion and good will. Heavenly worship is more than congregational religious excitement. My friend, heavenly worship will bring down the very atmosphere of heaven to earth. Heavenly worship will draw the presence of God, which alone can eternally change a man or woman's heart for the good.

Sadly, some have claimed that they have created worship songs that have *caused heaven to meet earth*. Words are cheap. The movement that this music has been birthed out of is a very "easy going" carnal, worldly, youth movement that winks at sins and stresses the free grace of God. The leadership of this movement is sensual and vain and will justify in a thousand ways their false liberty.

Heavenly Dancers Needed

I used to minister at one of the largest churches on the East Coast until the carnal pastor and his wife kept pushing me to sing in the midst of a large group of female dancers. Don't get me wrong, I'm not against dance or female dancers. Some of the most beautiful expressions of worship to the Lord can be accomplished through the dance. Choreographed dance unto the Lord is also beautiful and uplifting—that is, if the people who are dancing are consecrated and are truly giving glory to God and not themselves! It is also important that when people dance to the Lord they should not try to dress provocatively or purposely draw attention to themselves. This hurts the cause of corporate worship more than it helps.

His presence cannot transform us if we are not attracting His presence. The antediluvian people of Noah's day repulsed God's presence. In this late hour, we too must be careful not to harbor sin and evil imaginations, which in fact will grieve and repulse God's presence.

And God saw that the wickedness of man was great in the earth, and that every imagination of the thoughts of his heart was only evil continually. And it repented the LORD that he had made man on the earth, and it grieved him at his heart.

(Genesis 6:5–6)

Heavenly worship is born out of a holy and humble disposition of heart, which naturally attracts the presence of God.

Through our own strength, we cannot reach up high enough to bring heaven down to earth, for we need God's grace in order to exercise heavenly worship. There are biblical conditions and patterns that must be carefully followed before glory will come down from heaven. (See 1 John 2:27.) And only the Holy Spirit of grace can teach us how to worship in a manner that is pleasing to God. How does one experience the presence of God in heavenly worship? Falling down at His feet, and adoring and worshipping Him with humility of heart is a good start. For in the kingdom of heaven, the way to reach up is to bow down. Our hearts must bow low before we can experience high worship.

Again, we must first realize that we are utterly dependant upon His grace and mercy to teach us how to worship as the angels worship in heaven. (See John 14:26.) For the Holy Spirit seeks to glorify Jesus and testify of Him. For the true spirit of worship will always originate from the Holy Spirit and will not ever exalt a person, however charismatic or gifted he might be. It is the spirit of worship that originates from heaven. Heavenly worship arises out of pure hearts that are humble and are passionate for God.

Thus, heavenly worship flows like a fountain from hearts that are separated unto God—hearts that are set aside from worldliness and sin. And heavenly worship will not flirt with another, nor will it receive what the world has to offer—for pure hearts will not "worship" at the secular movie house in this late hour. There are many spiritual "Israelites" who love to be scintillated at the groves, high places, and brass altars of the Philistines. Their hearts have become too full of the rubbish and evil imaginations of Hollywood.

However, heavenly worship ascends into a different realm. It ascends up the holy mount. It has pure eyes that can see the glory of God. It does not defile itself with any unclean thing. It has not become spiritually blind and deaf to the voice of God in this hour.

Noble Worship

It is now time for the bride to practice her heavenly protocol. She must learn heavenly decorum and study celestial virtue and nobility. She must learn how to approach the King. She must love purity and faithfulness. For the bride that Jesus is coming for is a worshipful bride. It is a bride that practices heavenly worship.

Heavenly worship loves God's Word and understands it spiritually. It can only be generated from hearts that have been truly born again and washed in the blood of Jesus. The Father only considers hearts that are washed in the atoning blood of Jesus to be holy and clean.

Elegant Worship

Heavenly worship is without selfish motives. Heavenly worship seeks only to exalt Christ out of a humble heart. Heavenly worship does not care to be seen of men. Heavenly worship will attract angels and the Holy Spirit, who then lifts the pure worshipper into heavenly scenery and a fresh vision from God. Heavenly worship loves quiet and solitude before the Lord. Its chief fruit is tranquility and peace. It shuns the seductive, brash, and raucous sounds of hell and the worship of Jezebel. Heavenly worship allows the Holy Spirit to "fire up" an anointed imagination, and upon it will paint fresh, visual impressions of the glory realm.

Worship for the Bride

Heavenly worship approaches God

reverently and prayerfully. You cannot "sashay and saunter" into a holy place where even angels enter lightly. This book's purpose is to capture a tiny foretaste of what is to come. The project isn't as much about music as it is about bringing the body of Christ into a *purer* form of worship—holy, fiery, seraphic worship that will help prepare the church in spiritual truth as the bride of Christ awaits her beloved Bridegroom in this final hour. Like John the Baptist, the bride will learn to hear His voice and to rejoice at the sound of the Bridegroom.

He that hath the bride is the bridegroom: but the friend of the bridegroom, which standeth and heareth him, rejoiceth greatly because of the bridegroom's voice.

(John 3:29)

That he might sanctify and cleanse it with the washing of water by the word, that he might present it to himself a glorious church, not having spot, or wrinkle, or any such thing; but that it should be holy and without blemish.

(Ephesians 5:26–27)

Holy Passion

Heavenly worship praises God with reckless abandon and with holy passion. *Song of Angels* was primarily produced for the remnant of believers who have an appetite for the presence of God. All too many precious believers have of late become virtually nauseated by some of the shallowness in regard to the praise and worship music "industry." God is grieved about it too! This isn't the first generation to whom God hasn't been pleased with the "worship offerings" and "sacrifices" arising from His church on planet earth.

I hate, I despise your feast days, and I will not smell in your solemn assemblies. Though ye offer me burnt offerings and your meat offerings, I will not accept them: neither will I regard the peace offerings of your fat beasts. Take thou away from me the noise of thy songs; for I will not hear the melody of thy viols. But let judgment run down as waters, and righteousness as a mighty stream. (Amos 5:21–24)

As it was in the days of Amos, heavenly

worship is about holiness, righteousness, and judgment in the heart. Worship should be more than "hype and glitter." True heavenly worship is intensely relational. It is more than showing exterior emotions or hitting a religious "high" that comes from an exciting new song. It is far more than "stage presence" or choreography! For genuine heavenly worship does not just involve an outward act; it truly requires that the whole life is totally consecrated to God.

> *I therefore urge you, brothers, in view of God's mercies, to offer your bodies as living sacrifices that are holy and pleasing to God, for this is a reasonable way for you to worship. Do not be conformed to this world, but continually be transformed by the renewing of your minds so that you may be able to determine what God's will is—what is proper, pleasing, and perfect.*
> (Romans 12:1-2 ISV)

In a Vision of the Night I Saw

By the way, *all believers* (regardless of age, race, ethnicity, culture, education, etc.) can have spiritual vision and have visions and dreams.

> *And it shall come to pass in the last days, saith God, I will pour out of my Spirit upon all flesh: and your sons and your daughters shall prophesy, and your young men shall see visions, and your old men shall dream dreams.* (Acts 2:17)

God still gives visions and dreams and songs in the night. Through a holy and consecrated life; through glorious, pure worship, we can scale the lofty heights of Sinai and Horeb to receive a clear vision of God. This is not only to receive a new direction for our own lives but because through such an encounter others too will find purpose, provision, and impartation from the Lord as a result of our having sought Him so earnestly. The Holy Spirit is a person of vision and He rubs off on others. As a matter of fact, in Hebrew the word *anointing* means to "smear" or "rub upon a thing."

In a vision of the night, God can "seal" our instruction and pattern for ministry. For worship is about the whole life.

We should worship God and seek Him wherever we can find Him. This search should include not only the written Word, but also our prayer time and even our dreams. We should seek Him when we are awake and when we are asleep! Visions and dreams are an important aspect of our worship life as believers. The question remains, are you open and sensitive to the gentle, prophetic promptings of the Holy Spirit?

And he said, Hear now my words: If there be a prophet among you, I the LORD will make myself known unto him in a vision, and will speak unto him in a dream.

(Number 12:6)

In a dream, in a vision of the night, when deep sleep falleth upon men, in slumberings upon the bed; then he openeth the ears of men, and sealeth their instruction. (Job 33:15–16)

In your worship, are you open to the fact that angels are standing nearby, ready to serve you in Jesus' name?

And I said, Let them set a fair mitre upon his head. So they set a fair mitre upon his head, and clothed him with garments. And the angel of the LORD stood by. And the angel of the LORD protested unto Joshua, saying, Thus saith the LORD of hosts; If thou wilt walk in my ways, and if thou wilt keep my charge, then thou shalt also judge my house, and shalt also keep my courts, and I will give thee places to walk among these that stand by.

(Zechariah 3:5–7)

Like Joshua, we too must become hungry and thirsty for God. We too must love His commandments and walk steadfastly in the fruit of the Holy Spirit.

The Song of Angels

And now it's our desire to worship the Lord together. In the last days, through the power of the Holy Spirit, God is giving His people visions and dreams. *Song of Angels* is also about visions and dreams of Jesus and heaven. The music and the message are but revelations of His beautiful nature. The Holy Spirit longs to speak of and exalt Jesus even as He did when

Christ walked upon the earth. And He is doing so even more frequently, especially in nations that have been closed to traditional gospel missions. The divine Paraclete, the Holy Spirit's presence upon the earth, will help us win the entire world to Christ.

But when the Comforter is come, whom I will send unto you from the Father, even the Spirit of truth, which proceedeth from the Father, he shall testify of me.

(John 15:26)

Since the ancient time of Jacob's visions and dreams (where he saw angels ascending and descending from heaven), to the revelation of Jesus Christ to the seven churches in Revelation, Christianity has been birthed by necessary and timely visions and dreams given to men and women of God. The Bible is replete with examples of great men and women of God having visitations from heaven and incredible visions and dreams.

And he dreamed, and behold a ladder set up on the earth, and the top of it reached to heaven: and behold the angels of God ascending and descending on it.

(Genesis 28:12)

In a divinely inspired dream, Paul saw a man from Macedonia crying out for him to come over and help him. (See Acts 28:31.) The supernatural wonders of the Holy Spirit are still present in the church today. We simply need to get quiet before the Lord and make ourselves available to Him. Jesus is the same, yesterday, today, and forever! (See Hebrews 13:8.)

King David saw the power and glory of God in the sanctuary. But God is no respecter of persons. He can appear or give a vision or dream not only to a great patriarch of Israel or a first-century church apostle, but also to ordinary people such as the shepherds who were keeping flock by night.

And suddenly there was with the angel a multitude of the heavenly host praising God, and saying, Glory to God in the highest, and on earth peace, good will toward men. (Luke 2:13–14)

The great king and prophet of Israel, David, continually cried out with a heart of worship that said, "I want to see God. I want to see His throne in heaven."

I have seen you in the sanctuary and beheld your power and your glory.

(Psalm 63:2 NIV)

Many other prophets and sincere believers have seen into heaven while still alive on this earth. God doesn't require everyone to die before they can see Jesus. He only requires us to have pure hearts.

God blesses those whose hearts are pure, for they will see God.

(Matthew 5:8 NLT)

A Song in the Night

And God gives visions and songs in the night!

In thoughts from the visions of the night, when deep sleep falleth on men.

(Job 4:13)

In a dream, in a vision of the night, when deep sleep falleth upon men, in slumber-ings upon the bed.

(Job 33:15)

Yet the LORD will command his lovingkindness in the daytime, and in the night his song shall be with me, and my prayer unto the God of my life.

(Psalm 42:8)

Everyone who sees the Son of God for who He is through the Scriptures and believes on Him may have eternal life—that is the Good News! But I have some more good news. You don't necessarily need to *die physically* in order to see the glorified Jesus! Didn't Saul, Stephen, and John see him while they still breathed earth's air? Didn't Moses, Aaron, and the seventy elders of Israel also see Him?

And they saw the God of Israel: and there was under his feet as it were a paved work of a sapphire stone, and as it were the body of heaven in his clearness. And upon the nobles of the children of Israel he laid not his hand: also they saw God.

(Exodus 24:10–11)

If you have never seen Jesus in a vision, that doesn't make you any less a Christian. But neither should it diminish our desire to see Him yet. Nor should we envy or question the validity of another true believer who has. For sooner or later, all will see Him.

> Verily I say unto you, There be some standing here, which shall not taste of death, till they see the Son of man coming in his kingdom. (Matthew 16:28)

> And the stars of heaven shall fall, and the powers that are in heaven shall be shaken. And then shall they see the Son of man coming in the clouds with great power and glory. And then shall he send his angels, and shall gather together his elect from the four winds, from the uttermost part of the earth to the uttermost part of heaven. (Mark 13:25–27)

> And Jesus said, I am: and ye shall see the Son of man sitting on the right hand of power, and coming in the clouds of heaven. (Mark 14:62)

An Angel's-Eye View

But we desperately need God's perspective regarding heavenly worship. In our worship, we need to secure heaven's outlook on things. Having an angelic perspective is of the utmost importance because once you have a vision of glory, you will ardently desire everyone you meet to be with Jesus there in that place. It will lead to greater fruit in personal evangelism because you will understand and recognize your true authority in Christ. Because you have a clear revelation that you are seated in heavenly places with Christ Jesus, you will dare to do anything in Christ's name.

PART II–THE MUSIC

When God Comes Near

The whole purpose of worship is for us to draw near to God. *"Draw near to God and He will draw near to you"* (James 4:8 NKJV). *"Let us draw near with a true heart in full assurance of faith, having our hearts sprinkled from an evil conscience and our bodies washed with pure water"* (Hebrew 10:22 NKJV).

There are many wonderful benefits to blessing the Lord, but these are just a natural by-product of walking continually in the presence of God through a life of worship. Jesus should be the sole focus of our worship at all times.

The Benefits of Our Worship

Experiencing His sweet presence on earth is only a foretaste of the glories that are to come. When we begin to see our Bridegroom for who He truly is and begin to worship Him purely, He will reveal Himself to us in greater measure in this hour, for He is preparing for Himself a heavenly bride. Do you love Him with all your soul, mind, and heart? Heaven has a message for you: Your Bridegroom is coming! Prepare your heart! Get ready for the New Jerusalem to descend from heaven like a crystal, transparent, fiery jewel!

Angels in Paradise

To the listener: The following lyric notes have been written for prayerful meditation and reflection of certain scriptural truths. While listening to each song, we believe it is wise to read the lyrics and notes. We believe doing so will give the listener the most spiritual benefit.

Ocean (Intro)

Jon Devries/Freddy Hayler
© 2006 Golden Altar Records

Shores of Eternity

John DeVries, Rebekah Hayler
Vocals: Rebekah Hayler

Flowing water—healing;
Thunder—God's power and
authority; Birdcalls—paradisiacal
beauty; Harp—presence of angels;
Ocean—eternity

I Love to Praise Your Name

Mango
Arranged by Celso Valli
English lyrics adapted by Freddy Hayler

In the morning when I wake up
In the evening when I rise
I will lift my hands to heaven
I will lift them to the sky
I know that You're there
I know that You care
I need Your sweet presence
How I love to praise Your name,
Lord
You're the lover of my soul
You're the One that calms my
heart, Lord
You're the Savior of my soul
I know that You're there
I know that You care
And when You are near me
There is no fear when You are near
That's why I sing
I love to praise Your name, Lord
The lover of my soul
I love to praise Your name, Lord
Oh let Your Spirit take control
Let my heart and soul become
A special song unto You

A holy fragrance
So when I pray
I'll hear You say
How much You love me
I love to sing Your praises
Like a knight in shining armor
Brighter than a million stars
You are coming soon from heaven
Coming for Your lovely bride
When I am glad
When I am sad
When I am lonely
I'll fly away
To a high place
That's why I sing
I love to praise Your name, Lord
The Healer of my soul
I love to praise Your name, Lord
Oh may Your Spirit take control
Let my heart and soul become
A special song unto You
A holy fragrance
So when I pray
I'll hear You say how much You
love me
I love to praise Your name, Lord
Forever I will praise Your name
How I love to praise Your name

From "L'Attesa" © 2004 Sugar Music S.p.A.
Ed.Mus. S.r.l © 2006 Published in USA by
Sugar- Melodi, Inc./Chrysalis Music Group

A HOLY FRAGRANCE

Liberta ("Liberty")

Francesco Sartori—Alessio Bonomo
Arranged by Celso Valli, Francesco Sartori,
Giancarlo Di Maria
English lyrics adapted by Freddy Hayler

Let my heart run free
Free to worship You
Give me liberty
To ascend on high
Set Your people free
That they all may see You
Riding on a bright white horse
With wings of gentle light
To a place in paradise
Please take me
Far above the clouds
Of earthly trials and toils and pain
To a place of peaceful bliss
In the Father
Take me to that place
I love You, Father
Please take me now, Lord
I feel Your Spirit wind
Gently stir my soul
Fill me now within
Heal and make me holy
Keeper of the far wind that blows
I feel Your gentle breeze

Running through the willow trees
In Your garden
People are running free
Across a peaceful field
It's a place that's more than real
Forever
Take me to that place
I love You, Father
Please take me now, Lord
Lift me now, Lord
Keeper of the moon and stars
The Maker of my form
You're the One who calms the
storm
In my soul
I see the green hills
And I hear a gentle melody
Roll across the glassy sea
A constellation
Of the beauty of Your love
I love You, God!
Please lift me up
Liberta, Liberta!

Carry Me There

Guy Chambers—Enrique Iglesias
Alessandra Scuri—Beatrice Quattrini
English adaptation by Freddy Hayler

And I know that your motto
Is, Praise the Lord
Yet I know you're really
Feelin' kinda sore
Cause deep inside
I know your mind
Is really reeling from side to side
You keep saying
Lord
Why have You left me here?
Lord
Can You see me crying all alone
Down here
And Lord
Can You lend a hand
God please help me
To reach the Promised Land
Lord, I will cast my care
Lord, pick up this load
And carry me there
God, make me a man
That You can trust
No matter what comes my way
I'll be righteous and just

And if I fall
Even seven times
Please lift me up, Lord
So I can stand and fight
Lord
Your grace is far greater than
Lord
Greater than he that's in the world
And Lord
Can You lend a hand
God, please help me
To reach the Promised Land
Lord, now I will cast my care
Lord, lift up this load
And carry me there
O God I really need You now
Don't let the devil take control!
O God
I really need Your love and grace
I need Your love and grace, Lord
Lord
Can You lend a hand
God, please help me
To reach the Promised Land
Lord, now I will cast my care
On Your big shoulders
Please carry me there
Lord
Make me a man

That You can trust, Lord
To reach that Promised Land
Lord, help me to stand
Lord, lift up this load
And carry me there
Lord, please carry me there

I Need You Now (Psalm 51)

Watson/Saggese/Vergnaghi
Lyrics and English adaptation by Freddy Hayler

Jesus, You know how I love You
Never would I want to grieve You
Come now and heal me
And wash me in clean waters
You always lift me when I fall
You are so gentle and faithful
Give me Your heart and Your mind
To see
The ways of Your love and grace
Cause me to know
O God don't take away Your Spirit,
Lord
God give me grace
And cast me not away from Your
presence
Lord
I need You now, O God
Wash me in Your own blood
Purge all my sins away
Draw me with tender love
You are so holy and mighty
Do not, Lord, give me what I seek
But blot out my sins and
transgressions
The precious cleansing blood

Of Your own dear Son
Oh holy God of fire
Come fill me now
Come purify my heart
From everything that grieves You
now
That would offend You, Lord
Purify my whole mind
Cleanse me and purify
I give You my whole heart!
Lord, take all this heart of stone
Make me Your very own
I give You my whole heart!

Prevail

Laurex—Raffaello Di Pietro
English lyrics adapted by Freddy Hayler

*Yea, and all that will live godly in Christ
Jesus shall suffer persecution.*
(2 Timothy 3:12)

To my dear brothers and sisters around the world who are now facing severe persecution—paradise awaits every faithful believer. My friend, endure suffering and persecution with joy and thanksgiving, knowing that you are filling up the full cup of your reward in heaven. Simply yield to the Holy Spirit, and Christ will prevail in you!

Jesus said, "*Blessed are you when they revile and persecute you*" (Matthew 5:11).

The spirit of "Prevail" that was firmly rooted in the early church was also resonant in the consecrated heart of Madame Guyon, who said,

In vain they smite me. Men but do what God permits with different view; to outward sight they wield the rod, but faith proclaims it all of God.

Unmoved, then, let me keep thy way, supported by that cheering ray, which, shining distant, renders clear."

148

Verse 1

You can say what you want
While you act spiritual
You can gossip and talk
You can try and find fault
But you'll never prevail
Even persecute me. . .
Or take away all I own
You can do what you please
In your prideful disease
But you'll never prevail
Cause down deep in my heart
There's a Savior inside of me
My foundation and hope
You see is indestructible. . .

Chorus 1

There is a mansion
Prepared for me
It doesn't matter
What the enemy seeks
For there is victory
In Christ our Lord
I'm His sanctuary
I am a temple
Not made by men
And though they burn and
Shoot this outer man

Verse 2

You see, He's Lord of my temple
I'm burning bright with His love
And He'll never forsake me
He'll perform that within me
Complete His work in my heart
Through the coming storm clouds
And all the wind and the rain
My foundations are deep
I've hid His Word in my heart
His righteousness will prevail.
Non e un canto di addio
[This is not a farewell song]
Ma una musica dolce
[But sweet music]
Un orchestra che io
[An orchestra I play]
Suono solo per Te
[Just for You]

Chorus 2

There is a gold crown
Laid up for me
A place to dwell in on the Crystal
Sea
He'll never leave me or forsake my
heart
And Jesus will prevail...

NEVER FORSAKEN

Nothing can keep me from
His pure love
That flows so richly from
His throne above
And soon He's coming for
His faithful bride
Lord, find me resting in
Your love and grace...
And very soon I'll hear the trump
of God
And I will ascend on High...

ASCEND

Elijah II

L. Dalla
English lyrics adapted by Freddy Hayler

Only the Spirit of Elijah (the Holy Spirit) can bring about a heaven-sent revival in this hour. A technologically advanced, humanistic, and arrogant generation can only be moved by a display of powerful holiness preaching with miracles, signs, and wonders confirming God's Word.

Verse 1

I see amber horses
Ascending in the desert sky
Bright chariots of fire
Burning in a whirlwind
A man is crying
My Father, My Father
As he holds his veil
By the River Jordan

Chorus 1

Farewell, Elijah!
Farewell, my father Elijah!
For I lay my mantle down
God send down the spirit of Elijah

Verse 2

Veo la gente llorando
[I see people crying]
Para paz y pureza
[For more peace and purity]
Ellos teinen hambre
[They are all hungry]
Tienen sed en el corazon
[And they are thirsty in their hearts]
Y lloran para mas de Dios
[They are crying out for more of God]
Miran a las estrellas del cielo
[They look up and see the stars of God's heaven]
Estan listos en su corazon
[They are ready in their hearts]

Verse 3

Miramos al cielo
[Let us look to God's heaven]
Para ver Su Luz
[And see His bright coming]
Mirar mas alla de las estrellas
[To look beyond the stars]
Ver Cristo en nuestro corazon
[To see Christ in our hearts]
Y amarlo totalmente
[And love Him totally]

PAZ Y PUREZA

Amarlo con todo el corazon
[And love Him with all the heart]
El corazon
[With all of my heart]
Como Noah, se separan de pecados
[Like Noah, they depart from sin]
Entregan todo a Cristo
[They surrender all to Christ]
Entregan todo a Cristo
[They surrender all to Christ]

Chorus 2

Send down the spirit of Elijah!
For I lay my mantle down
Send down the fire of Elijah!

Verse 4

As the Holy Spirit
Divides the true from the false
As His angelic reapers
Separate the wheat from the tares
Purify your altars
Tear the god of mixture down
And weep before His altar
For false shepherds and their
prophets
Who for ambition's sake
Devour the souls of the innocent
Who wink at sin

And trifle with evil
O precious bride of Christ
Put on clean garments of holiness
Come and separate yourselves
From Baal's sin and worldliness

Chorus 3

God of all power
I hear the voice of Elijah's call
Consume all evil now
Send down the fire of Elijah
God of Elijah
Send down the fire of Elijah
Consume all evil now
Send down the fire of revival!

Jesus speaking...

Oh beloved
I am coming
For My bride
Without spot or wrinkle
Pure and holy
Unto Me
Prepare your hearts...in My love
and purity

From "Caruso"
Publishing: Ed. BMG Ariola Spa/Assist S.r.l
Published in USA © 2001
2004 BMG Music Publishing/EMI Music
Publishing

The Priestly Bride

Dedicated to our dear sister in Christ, Anna Rountree, who has been to heaven many times. Thank you for sharing with us your beautiful visits there...

Pier Paolo Guerrini—Giorgio Calabrese
English lyrics adapted by Freddy Hayler

Verse 1

(**Freddy**)

You
So merciful and kind
So holy and so pure
Are causing me to see divinely
You
Like a starry night that shines
My eyes are drawn to You
As You bring healing to my mind and soul
I feel Your love and the angels' dew
And hear the song of the angels

Chorus 1

(**Freddy**)

To sing the Song of Angels
To sing a song divine
To stand here in Your presence

This is my prayer, my whole desire
Like music on a breeze
My heart flows unto You
In a symphony of praise to You
In worship to My God

Verse 2

(Rebekah)

Lord Jesus, You're my life and hope
I'll be Your priestly bride
And I will live my life for You
In purity and holiness
In righteousness and truth
I await the day
When underneath the canopy
We'll be joined as one

(Freddy)

I await the day

Interlude

Verse 3

(Rebekah)

See
That precious little girl

SONG OF ANGELS

153

Whose heart does safely trust
So innocent and clearly Yours and too
I want to trust like this
As I release my heart
Forever to be Yours and chosen

Chorus 2

(Freddy and Rebekah)

For the great day when You come from heaven
To carry me far above that starry night

(Freddy)

Lord Jesus, You're my destiny
I'll be Your priestly bride
I know You're coming soon for me

(Rebekah)

O Lord

(Freddy and Rebekah)

Our love is for all time

When time shall be no more
I'll just fly away

Together for eternity
I'll gaze into Your eyes
So whenever I get lonely
I'll sing the Angel Song
And soar into the heavenlies
This is my prayer, my whole desire
Like music on a breeze my heart
My heart flows unto You
In a symphony of praise to You
In worship to My God
And then I heard an angel ask,
Who is this lovely bride?
It is the priestly bride
Of Christ!

From "L'Abitudine" © 2001, 2004—Melodi Casa Editrice S.r.1 Published in USA by Sugar-Melodi, Inc./Chrysalis Music Group

Testimony

Pietro Mascagni—Marioni-Luigino Biagioni—Carlo Botteghi
English lyrics adapted by Freddy Hayler

If it were not for the grace of God, I would not be here to sing or write the words to this song. Yet, it was some time after my conversion that I truly came to appreciate and comprehend the following Scripture from the prophet Ezekiel.

And when I passed by thee, and saw thee polluted in thine own blood, I said unto thee when thou wast in thy blood, Live; yea, I said unto thee when thou wast in thy blood, Live. (Ezekiel 16:6)

Verse 1

Lord, I sing this song unto You because
You are so glorious
You're so loving so true and so kind
To reach down and touch me
With Your love
And I'll never forget the day
When You caused me to live

I was dying inside from my sinfulness
Insecure, full of fear and rejected of all men
No one cared for my soul
Polluted as I lay in my blood
When on a warm summer night I cried out
To a God that I really didn't know
Then You and Your great love came down
And took me in Your arms
I remember what You said to me
Of Your everlasting love for me

Chorus 1

And now I sing "You are so glorious"
Jesus, You're so glorious
Of all the music of my heart, oh let pure worship arise
Oh my God, oh how I love You
God, how I adore You
Well, it was sometime later I learned that
Once You were also alone
Were rejected of all and despised by all men
Were abused, beaten, and hung on

a cross
Left to die
No one cared for Your soul as they mocked You
They cast lots for Your robe as Your blood flowed
In fear You cried out, "Oh My God, why have You forsaken me?"
As the lightning and thunder of God's wrath resounded all around
As warm tears of great love rained down and mixed with the blood-soaked ground
I was with You in that moment
When You took my sins upon You

Chorus 2

And now I sing "You are so glorious"
Jesus, You're so glorious
Oh let sweet music of my praise and let pure worship arise
Oh my God, oh how I love You
God, how we adore You
Oh my God, how we love You
God, there's none beside You
Oh my God, I love You!

Consecrated Vessel

Francesco Sartori – Lucio Quarantotto

In the beginning of the world
All was dark and void without form
Till Your Spirit breathed life into all
The breath of Your life
For it was love that gave the light
Oh it was pure love
When You created
The sun and moon and stars
And all the galaxies
In a realm far too large to conceive
But it was great love
When You looked down and called
my name
Lord it was pure love
When You set fire to my soul
Sweet Lord
Your Spirit
Gave life to my soul
How can I thank You
But to give my life, my all
May I forever be
A temple holy
A consecrated vessel
So those who dwell in the dark
May receive the light of God
That they may see salvation in You
Please send Your light, Lord

Into their darkened lives and
worlds
That all may know You
That they may come to see You,
Lord
Glory to God in the highest
To see the Son of God
Burning brightly like the sun
God, may they ever be
A temple holy
Consecrated vessel
Come quickly Jesus
Prepare Your people in Your love
Come bright and shining Knight
Come take Your bride arrayed in
white
God may we see descend
The new Jerusalem!
Descending from Your Throne
And all the nations flowing unto
You
I give my life to You
I give my all to You
A consecrated vessel
For You
For You

Garden in Paradise

Francesco Sartori—David Foster—Alessio Bonomo
English lyrics adapted by Freddy Hayler
New arrangement by Freddy Hayler

Garden in paradise
Rolling hills
Green-rolled lawns
Beds of colored flowers
Quiet pools
Fragrant trees
Streams of life are flowing
Stairs of light
Angels bright
Emanating, glowing,
Joyfully
Laughingly
Lead me to His garden
To paradise on high
My spirit longs to fly
To the brilliance of His
Glory and His light
Jesus, You're my heart's desire
I long to see Your sweet face
And run to Your loving embrace
My Jesus
Lover of my soul
Jesus, You're my heart's desire

And I will wait for You here
In the midst of Your garden of love
And worship till You come unto me

Interlude

Cinnamon
Frankincense
Calamus, sweet aloes
Beautiful,
Tree of life,
Center of His Temple
I feel strong
Full of life
Youthfulness and pure joy
Gentle breeze,
Garden walls
Tall white marbled columns
Garden in paradise
My Spirit longs to fly
As angels of His Presence
Open up the gate
Jesus enters paradise
In all His splendor and grace
The light rays and beams
From His face
He gazes,
With eyes of liquid, pure love
Stunned by love, as I'm crying out,
Son of God!

Jesus, clothed with robes
Of pure light
Bright diamonds sparkle and shine
In a rainbow of colorful light
My Jesus,
Oh to embrace my true love
Garden in paradise
Such beauty in
His garden of love
My Jesus,
Oh to embrace my true love,
Garden in paradise

*From "Chiara" © 2001, 2004—Sugar Sri/One
Four Three Music (Peermusic} LTD
© 2006 Published in USA by Sugar-Melodi,
Inc./Chrysalis Music Group*

The Visitation

Zdenek—Giorgi Calabrese
English lyrics adapted by Freddy Hayler

See
The edges of the air afire,
A searing Light and heavenly choir
As angels fill my room
See
A glorious swirling cloud descend
It's burning brighter with His glory
Now
And He comes to me. . .
The burning air
Begins to swell as His presence
nears
Angels sweetly sing
Beautiful
So beautiful
Now I can see into His eyes
An endless pool of liquid love
And now I know He's mine
Love
A love too deep for words
If you could travel into His eyes
You would know all mysteries
Jesus
Rose of Sharon, fairest of
Ten thousand angels from Your

Throne above
And You bid me come
Bright colors of love
Are beaming forth from Your lovely
face
Spring air and sweet fragrance
Of Your grace
Such Majesty
I'm all ablaze with His life
Now I am one with His fiery love
It forever burns in my heart

Interlude

Oh how He loves you too
And I am one with Him
And all ablaze with His love
And when He bids me to come...
I'm forever with Him...

From "E mi Manchi Tu"
© 2001, 2004—Sugar Music SPA/Double
Marpot Edizioni Musicali—Published in USA
by Sugar-Melodi, Inc./Chrysalis Music Group

The Temple of God

Francesco Sartori—David Foster—Lucio Qurantotto, Claudio Corradini
English lyrics adapted by Freddy Hayler

Verse 1

Angels dressed in lavender
Bring me to the temple of God
To a clear, blue pool
Reflecting light
I dip into
Clean waters of life
And as I ascend I see burning
A brazen altar of sacrifice
Seven gold lamps illuminating
The table of showbread and wine

Chorus 1

Then I hear the angels singing,
Holy
Holy, Holy is the Lamb of God
As choirs of angels sing and dance
before Him
I join the holy song to worship God

Verse 2

An altar of
Pure sweet incense
Smoke now fills
The temple of God

Fragrant aromas surround me
As I hear the angel song
Into the Holy of Holies
We proceed to the altar of God

Chorus 2

Then I hear the angels singing
Holy
Holy, Holy is the Lamb of God
His mercy seat and ark shine
bright before me
Shekinah rays and rainbows shine
and glow

Verse 3

Then a distant shofar sounds
Angels all around Him bow
The King of all the universe
On a white, steed galloping
descends to take me

Chorus 3

Master, Savior, King
My heart cries Holy
Holy, Holy is the Lamb of God

Dell'Amore (Love Now I Know)

Mauro Malavasi—Leo Z—Andrea Sandri
English lyrics adapted by Freddy Hayler

Arrestata mio cuore mia l'anima
You arrested my heart, my mind, and my soul
Amore che bella mia salvata
Your beautiful love saved me
Dimmi se a vero che lei esiste per davero
Tell me it's true that You are really there
Parla al mio cuore digli che sai
Speak to my heart
Dei miei dolori che non dormon mai
To my pain that never sleeps
Parlami o Dios e dimmi se lei verra
Speak, O God, tell me if You are coming for me
Vita fredda a distante
Life had seemed so distant and cold
Ma venisti a me
But You came to me
Va dove va l'amore
Angels plead with you
Angeli ti chiamano
The angels are calling you
Dell' amore lo so
Love, now I know You
Dell' amore lo so
Love, now I know You
Dell' amore lo so
Love, now I know!
Angels of heaven now carry my prayer to God
It was late fall when the first winter winds
Blew very coldly
There was darkness within
I could not see a warm light out on the horizon
But You looked down from heaven
Came to draw me
Your great love arrested
My heart and my mind and my soul
God I love You with all my heart
God I love You with all my soul
God I love You with all my mind
God I love You with all my soul
Dell'amore lo so!
Dell'amore lo so!
tutto cambiera
All now will change
tutto rivivra
And all who love You will live
con te
with You

© 2004 Sugar S.r.l—Almud Ed. Mus. S.r.l—Double Marpot Ed. Mus. © 2006 Published in USA by Sugar-Melodi, Inc./Chrysalis Music Group

Moses

David Marjo Reyes
Arranged by Celso Valli
English lyrics and adaptation by Freddy Hayler

In the desert wind
I hear a still voice calling
In the desert night
I hear a whole nation cry
How long O God
How long O God
Till You deliver us?
For forty years
Moses prepared his heart in God
In a desert wilderness
Then through a burning bush
God gave to him a plan
To lead His captive people
To the Promised Land
And God said
Moses
Moses
Set My people free!
With God's rod in hand
He went down to Pharaoh's land
And with God in his mouth
He said, "Listen, Pharaoh"
Listen to God's command
Let My people go!

Let My people go!
To worship in the Promised Land!
God breathed the mighty wind
And the Red Sea did depart
And God's people rejoiced and
They passed into a safe place
Moses stood on high
And raised the rod of God
And the enemies of the Lord
Would be heard no more
Then the people cried
Moses
Moses
Moses
A true prophet sent from on high!
But a greater than Moses
Is standing near you now
The very Son of God from heaven
Came down
Into Jerusalem
Where the people cried out loud
Hosanna in the highest
Messiah
Savior
Then the people cried
Hosanna!
Hosanna!

All or Nothing

Guard—Rice
Lyrics adapted by Freddy Hayler

Vain, self-centered, Westernized, materialistic Christianity is neither hip nor relevant with Jesus. It's time to stop playing church and totally surrender our lives to service for Him. (See Romans 12:1-2.)

You always come to Me and pray
Just to get what you want or need
And when you pray to Me this way
I never hear a word you say
My friend will you listen to Me?
Will you really listen to Me?
Give Me all your heart
Give Me all your heart
All or nothing
Give Me all
Or nothing
Give Me all
Or nothing
Now's the time to surrender to Me
Now's the time to surrender to Me
You say, O Lord, this is too much
To let You be the Lord of all
When you come to Me one day
And say all the things you did

In My name
I will say I never knew you
Say I never knew you
Or can you hear My voice today?
Give Me all your heart
Give Me all your heart
All or nothing
All or nothing
Give Me all
Or nothing
Now's the time to surrender to Me
Now's the time to surrender to Me
I will fill You with My love and grace
I will send My Spirit to you
Surrender all

Chariots of Angels

F. Sartori—L. Quarantotto
English lyrics and adaptation by Freddy Hayler

The good men perish; the godly die before their time, and no one seems to care or wonder why. No one seems to realize that God is taking them away from evil days ahead. For the godly who die shall rest in peace. (Isaiah 57:1-2 TLB)

Verily, verily, I say unto you, Except a corn of wheat fall into the ground and die, it abideth alone: but if it die, it bringeth forth much fruit. (John 12:24)

And it came to pass, as they still went on, and talked, that, behold, there appeared a chariot of fire, and horses of fire, and parted them both asunder; and Elijah went up by a whirlwind into heaven. (2 Kings 2:11)

(Freddy)

Quando sono solo
[When I'm all alone]
Sogno all'orizzonte
[I dream on the horizon]
Mancan le parole
[And words fail.]
Si lo so che non c'e luce
[Yes, I know there is no light]
luna stanza quando
[Or hope in a room where]
Manca il sole
[The sun is absent.]
Say what you say,
To comfort me, please

(Rebekah)

Still, I don't know,
Why God took you so young
So prime
In your glory
I hear what they say, but mystery
Still shrouds why the Lord took
you.

Chorus 1

(Rebekah)

Jesus carry me
On chariots of angels
Where I can see
The beauty and glory of God
His garden in paradise

Chariot come swing low
Soon the day will come
When we will go
On chariots of angels on high
To gardens in paradise

Verse 2

(Freddy)

Tutto solo nel mio letto
[But I am all alone in my bed]
Ho pianciuto, tutta notte
[Weeping tears all night,]
I just turned around,
Now they say you're gone my friend
But it won't be long
Before I'll see you soon again

Chorus 2

(Rebekah)

Jesus carry me
On chariots of angels
Where I can see
The beauty and glory of God
His garden in paradise
Jesus let me see
The glories of heaven
The Crystal Sea

On chariots of angels on high
His garden in paradise
Jesus carry me
On chariots of angels
Where I can see
Lo con te!
[I with you again]

From "Con te Partiro"
Publishing C 1995, 2004 Insieme S.r.l/Double Marpot Ed. Musicali
© 2006 Sugar-Melodi, Inc./Chrysalis Music Group

Song of Angels (Outro)

Rebekah and Freddy Hayler
Malise English Lyrics: Freddy Hayler

Io, vorrei (I desire); liberarti (to
liberate you); dpmattina (at dawn);
e vorrei (and would like); vederti
volare (to see you fly); un carro
d'angelo (on chariots of angels);
al cielo (on high); Tu (you); El
Padre Santo (with the Holy Father);
Espiritu Santo (with the Holy
Spirit); angelico (like an angel);
el l'anima (and the soul); se ne
va (departs) verso l'eternita (to
eternity); Gloria! (Glory!)

Tongues of fire...
Tongues of angels...

Credits

Producer: *Freddy Hayler*
Soundtrack and Musical Arrangement: *John DeVries, Larry Hall, Steve Errante, Freddy Hayler*
Package Design and Layout: *Ford Design*
Photography: *Brownie Harris Photography, New York, NY and Wilmington, NC, Marshall Marvelli*
Transcription Production: *Freddy Hayler, Steve Errante, Larry Hall, and John DeVries*
Conceptual Design, Writing, and Editing: *Freddy and Anne Hayler*
Publishing: *Golden Altar Publishing, Song of Angels Publishing*
Chief Audio Engineer and Mix: *Dan Oxley/D&D Productions, Nashville TN*
Sound Engineers and Computer Programming: *J. K. Loftin, Wilmington, NC*
Additional Recording Studios: *David's Song Production, Nashville, TN*
Bobby Shin, Engineer, Nashville, TN
Mastering: *Benny Quinn, Masterphonics, Nashville, TN*

Clothiers: *Niel Flushman, Dennis Sugar and The Woody Wilson Collection*
Musicians Contractor: *David's Song Production/Nashville String Machine*
Strings: *David Davidson/ Concert Master*
Violin: *Alan Umstead, David Angell, Janet Askey, Karen Winklemann, Zebena Bowers, Bruce Christensen, Catherine Umstead, Pamela Suxfin*
Viola: *Idalynn Besser, Monisa Angell*
Cello: *Bob Mason, Lynn Peithman, Bradley Mansell*
Piano: *Rolin Mains*
Lead Guitar: *Paul Brannon*
Trumpet: *Jeff Bailey*
Oboe and English Horn: *Bobby Taylor, Roger Weismeyer*
Clarinet: *Matthew Davich*
Harp: *Mary Hoepfinger*
Percussion: *Mike Mann*
Flute, Alto Flute, Piccolo: *Brendon McKinney*
French Horn: *Beth Beeson, Jennifer Kummer, Calvin Smith, Steve Patrick*
Conductor: *Bobby Taylor, John DeVries*

Special thanks to Steve and Sandy Errante and the Girls Choir of Wilmington.

CD, Front Cover Art, and Logo:
Don Perkins, Keith Parkinson, Foster R. Barker
Mailing Address:
Golden Altar Records
P. O. Box 10740
Wilmington, NC 28404 U. S. A.
Tel. 910-262-4137
Fax: 910-270-3240

Personal Management and International Representation:
Declare His Glory Ministries International
Kingdom Management (904) 646-2626
2222 Walkers Glenn Ln.
Jacksonville, FL 32246

Email: declaringHim@cs.com
Email: kingdommanagement@hotmail.com
Official Websites: www.songofangels.com
www.declareHisglory.org

Thank You's

All praise and honor to the Lord Jesus Christ, the King of Kings. For without His grace and guidance this project could never have been realized. Jesus, we love You with all of our hearts! I am so grateful to my wife, Annie—for her constant friendship, love, and encouragement. Without her prayers and intercession I would not have been able to complete this volume. To my precious daughters, Lindsay and Rebekah. You are the two most precious daughters a father could ever hope for.

I would like to say thanks to old friends and new friends alike. We are so grateful and appreciative to Anna and Albert Rountree. Thank you, Anna, for sharing your incredible experiences in the heavenly realms with us. Thanks to our friends Steve and Joy Strang for introducing them to us!

To Gwen Shaw and the End-Time Handmaidens—much appreciation for your prayers, faithful support, and encouragement. Thanks to John and Helena Kelly and Ed Mannering, our kind and caring friends from the "nation" called Texas. To Bob and Rose Weiner—doers of the Word and true friends who love the message of holiness and who accomplish world missions.

To our dear friend in Orlando, Pastor Sam Hinn—a compassionate man of God with a heart to worship ["aye"—a very fine hockey player as well!] Jeffrey Levinson for playing the anointed shofar. Thanks to an old friend and great pastor, Lamar Sentell; to John and Anne Giminez who, after marrying us many years ago, still inspire and encourage our family. Thanks to Rick and Julie Joyner.

Thanks to Ford Design. To Dan Oxley and D&D Studios for a great mix! To John DeVries and Blair Masters for helping to create beautiful soundtracks.

And thanks to Sugar Melodi USA and Chrysalis Music; to Sugar Music, Milan, Italy—a gifted and ingenious group of talented songwriters who have produced the most beautiful, peaceful melodies on the planet! Thanks to Anne's mom and dad in Orlando and to my mom and family in Boston and in Providence, R.I.—we honor you! Tons of love and thanks to you all for your prayers.

—Freddy Hayler

Philippians 1:6